THE HILLWALKER'S MANUAL

*Looking to the impressive nose of Sgurr an Fhidhleir,
North West Highlands of Scotland*

CICERONE

2 POLICE SQUARE, MILNTHORPE, CUMBRIA, LA7 7PY
www.cicerone.co.uk

British Library Cataloguing-in-Publication Data. A catalogue record for this book is available from the British Library.

ACKNOWLEDGEMENTS

Thanks are due to all those with whom I've shared precious moments in the hills or who have assisted directly with this book: John Adams, Mike Ansel, Martin Battersby, Dave Birkett, John Cleare, Colin Downer, Joy Evans, Mike Feeley, Roy Garner, Rick Graham, Tony Greenbank, James Gregory, Fiona Fraser, John Hargreaves, Andy Hyslop, Susan Lund, Cameron McNeish, Fiona Mirrlees, Keefe Murphy, John Quine, Jane Renouf, Duncan Richards, Jon Rigby, Stewart Sykes, Mark Squires, John and Gill White and Stuart Wood.

For checking the manuscript I would like to thank Susan Birkett.

For the use of equipment, advice and personnel I would like to thank Rock and Run (Ambleside).

For the line drawings I would like to thank Martin Bagness.

Thanks to the Scottish Tourist Board and the Welsh Tourist Board for assistance with accommodation and Virgin Trains for travel assistance.

Thanks also to Lowe Alpine for the use of the clothing photographs on pp.44–45 and to Meindl and Bramwell International for the photographs and care information on boots and footware on pp.36–38 and Kohla for the walking pole photograph on p.89.

Front cover photograph: Swirl How in the English Lake District
Back cover photograph: a perfect autumn day on the Lakeland fells

13153099

CONTENTS

ABOUT THE AUTHOR

Lakeland native Bill Birkett is one of Britain's foremost mountain writers and photographers. A leading climber and hill walker, and a former civil engineer, he has spent a lifetime exploring the hills and wild places of the world. His breathtaking photography illustrates numerous publications and his own books include the best selling *Complete Lakeland Fells* and *Great British Ridge Walks*, *Classic Treks of the World* and his recent definitive guidbooks *Exploring The Lakes and Low Fells (Vols 1 and 2)*.

Bill Birkett is a member of the British Guild of Travel Writers, Fédération Européene Des Associations De Jornalists Du Tourisme, Outdoor Writers Guild (Committee), Society of Authors, and the Fell and Rock Climbing Club of the English Lake District.

FOREWORD

Hills attract and excite all free spirits. Those who accept their challenge, and tackle them correctly, will be rewarded – for the fascination of being on and exploring these high, wonderfully wild, places is something that, once experienced, will remain with you for life.

But the hills come in many forms and have moods that are distinct and change with the season and weather – the sunshine and warmth of summer can be found there, but so too can the white snows and biting cold of winter. Whatever the season, weather hastens change, and these changes add yet another dimension to this kaleidoscopic world. To appreciate the hills, to experience them at their best and enjoy them fully, one must know them a little; and whatever the conditions, you must wear and use the right equipment, must be able to find your way through them, must learn the essential fundamental techniques required to scale and traverse them, and must have an overall awareness of the concept of survival. These, then, form the constituent parts of this manual. And because so many people like to record their walks, and enjoy taking photographs, I have covered the basic points of successful hillwalking photography too.

This book is made up of six chapters covering the main subjects, with each chapter consisting of numerous modules of information. The intention is that these can be referred to separately and the whole picture structured as you wish.

If anyone should proffer the opinion that you do not need to learn the craft of hillsmanship let me refer you to some interesting facts. In mainland Britain alone, over a three-year period, the number of incidents dealt with by the mountain rescue services numbered a staggering 2,214. From these incidents arose 2,799 casualties and 316 fatalities. To ensure that you do not become one of those statistics I would advise you to learn the craft well.

I was very lucky to have been born in the hills and to be the son of a brilliant rock-climber, and hence much of my time has been spent climbing. Nevertheless I have never taken either the hills or my right to be there for granted. Safety, I was always taught, comes first – the 'mountains give and the mountains take' – and this should never be forgotten. Correct use of equipment and correct application of technique were always presented as a science and a craft needing both knowledge and practice. Experience is ultimately the great teacher and you learn most from your mistakes; but in the hills these mistakes should be small ones, and your learning must be both theoretical and practical.

Most of all, however, I have experienced great joy and freedom in the hills, and if this manual passes on something of my love, understanding and appreciation of them then I hope it will inspire you and serve you well.

Bill Birkett

Looking over a frozen tarn to Scafell (left) and Scafell Pike (right),
Three Tarns, Bowfell and the Western Fells of the Lake District.

THE HILLWALKER'S WORLD

Only a hill; yes, looked at from below,
Facing the usual sea, the frequent west;
Tighten the muscle, feel the strong blood flow,
And set your foot upon the utmost crest.
There, where the realms of thought and effort cease
Wakes on your heart a world of dreams and peace.
Geoffrey Winthrop Young

Hills hold a special place in the hearts of many walkers, and for us, it is enough simply to raise our eyes from the plains to realise that each hill has a character of its own. Primitively formed in most cases from rock, they exert a solid power and offer extremes of emotion with moods that change rapidly from kindly benevolence to brutal savagery at a blink of their weather eye. Above all they are quite simply magnificent.

Even within the small land area of Britain there is an incredible variety of hills: from the towering giants of remote Scotland through the rugged northern moors to the rolling and gentle downs of southern England. As great as their differences in height is the variety in their nature.

The hills you choose to venture upon may not be the highest or the toughest to climb, but to you they will always be unique. Hills can offer unparalleled pleasure and opportunity, whether they be a simple chalk ridge, humble but evocative, or an angry snow-clad lump of granite that looks down from lofty heights as if to say, 'Climb me if you can, if you dare'. The thrill and satisfaction of hillwalking is open to all those who are willing simply to put one foot in front of the other.

The challenge, excitement and thrill of scaling the heights is only one small aspect of hillwalking. For many it is enough to feel the freedom of the hills through the changing seasons and to enjoy the associated sights and sensations: the sweet autumnal smells and the dazzling colours of the leaves before they fall; the biting cold of winter, when nothing moves to break the frozen silence of an awesome black-and-white world; the yellows of the first spring flowers as nature begins to laugh again; those balmy summer days when a dip in the glacial mint-clear winters of a mountain stream brings instant healing to both body and mind.

Ben Nevis is Britain's highest mountain at 4406ft (1344m)

The distinctive chalk headland of the Seven Sisters, where the high chalk ridge of the South Downs falls into the English Channel

Hand in hand with this freedom comes the ultimate pleasure of solitude in a wilderness setting. Here is a world where you can be alone but never lonely, where life is so beautiful and full of wonder that it can never be imagined by those who confine themselves below. If you don't already go hillwalking, do make the effort, do feel the blood surge through your body: the hills are open to all.

'Only a hill': Looking tantalisingly attractive from below, Ben Nevis, Britain's highest mountain, holds many traps for the unwary. Weather conditions can deteriorate rapidly and its north face presents sheer cliffs of some 600 metres (2,000 feet). In winter, blizzards of arctic ferocity frequently plaster it with layers of snow and ice.

However, with these privileges must come responsibilities; to yourself, to others, to the environment. Never forget that hills can be both friendly and hostile: they can radically change in nature either because of prevailing weather conditions or the seasons. The higher they get the more difficult and serious they become: a walk in the hills that may be taken as a gentle stroll in summer can quickly become a mountaineering expedition and fight for survival in winter. Remember too, that altitude brings further problems of its own.

To be safe, to keep others safe and to preserve that delicate beauty, however fragile, awe-inspiring and grand it may seem, you must appreciate something of the physical nature of the hills. This chapter, then, examines the important and varied components that make up the upland environment in both summer and winter.

WEATHER AND THE SEASONS

One of the most important influences on the natural world is the weather – and hills attract its extreme variations. Given any hill walk of reasonable length and difficulty, the difference between an enjoyable outing and a grim struggle for survival (one which is lost by many hillwalkers each year) can simply be the prevailing weather conditions.

Any hillwalker should know the right techniques and have the right equipment to cope with any extreme conditions that might occur. You should be able to interpret weather forecasts correctly, and develop an understanding of the physical factors that determine the weather. The latter includes 'weather lore', the ability to read signs of change whilst actually on the hill. A detailed study of the weather would take another book, so here I will just illustrate some practical tips on how to interpret weather patterns while you are on the hill. It would be advisable, however, to read a more specialist book on the subject.

The interdependent, physical elements of 'weather' that most directly affect us are: temperature, sunshine level, precipitation and wind. To some extent these are predictably linked to the seasons. For example, on an average hill in the English Lake District in summer, you could expect anything from heavy rain to hot sunshine, but could predict with confidence that you would not meet snow or temperatures below freezing. But please note: I am not guaranteeing this to be the case!

A frosty morning and clear blue skies herald a perfect mountain day for these hardy winter campers at Wasdale Head, below Great Gable, the Lake District

11

Seasons

Seasons principally affect temperature and sunshine level and are, of course, dictated by the relative position of the earth to the sun. In Britain all four seasons can produce difficulties for the hillwalker:

- Winter: snow, ice, freezing cold conditions and the danger of hypothermia

- Spring: sudden showers and unpredictability

- Summer: warmth with a danger of extremes of heat, exhaustion and dehydration

Autumn colours outside a mountain inn. Whilst it may be warm and sunny at this altitude the tops of the high hills may already be frozen and clad in ice. The Brittania Inn, Elterwater, the Lake District

- Autumn: mists and fog and the possibility of getting lost; and again, unpredictability, with beautiful Indian summers one year, an early start to winter the next

In much the same way as the seasons were vitally important to prehistoric man (as witness Stonehenge and other stone circles constructed to read the sun's position) they are important to the hillwalker too – our well-being depends on our understanding them. Even though, or perhaps more correctly because, we live in a world of high technology and rapid communication, it is easy to forget the importance of understanding the basic elements of nature.

Whilst these are idealised images, and the actual weather pattern is somewhat more complicated, the effects of the seasons on the weather should always be appreciated. In Britain, generally speaking, May, June and September can be good months for the walker, giving dry settled spells and clear visibility. Winter walking is often best tackled in late February and early March as the days being to lengthen, and when snow and ice is most consolidated. August, October, November and December can often be the wettest months.

In the northern hemisphere the sunshine hours are at their longest in summer and shortest in winter. Whilst north of the Arctic Circle there is perpetual light in summer and darkness in winter, in Britain the hillwalker can expect (around midsummer) 18 hours of light and 6 hours of darkness (it stays lighter later the further north one travels). The opposite is true for winter, and whilst this may seem glaringly obvious the fact is that many hillwalkers are caught out by the shorter daylight hours of winter. The hillwalker should plan his day accordingly, with all consideration given to the daylight hours.

Temperature

Air and ground temperature, which can be significantly different, shape the hill environment. Its most immediately obvious control is over the form of precipitation: rain, sleet or snow (which all produce their own peculiar problems) can all occur with a temperature change of only a few degrees. Be aware, also, that a blisteringly hot day presents as many special problems as does a freezing cold day.

Generally temperature drops with altitude and this should be considered carefully by anyone going high. An average figure in Britain is that temperature drops 1°C for every increase in altitude of 150m. To bring this into perspective, the summit of Ben Nevis is on average approximately 9°C cooler than Fort William, the town at its foot.

Sunshine Level

The sunshine level determines not only the temperature but the hours of usable daylight. In summer guard against sunburn on all exposed parts including the oft-forgotten legs if wearing shorts. When travelling for extended periods over snow and ice protect the exposed vulnerable extremities from radiation burn as the sun's ultra-violet light is bounced back at you. Extra-strong sun-cream or, preferably, glacier cream is required on the lips, nose and eartips. Protect also against snow-blindness by wearing suitably tinted glacier goggles/spectacles.

Temperature inversion

Occasionally one experiences the phenomenon of temperature inversion – when the air is colder in the valleys than it is on the hills above. This occurs, notably, early in the day when clear skies above allow the sun to warm the hills whilst the valleys are still shrouded by heavy mist. In some instances you can leave the cloud below and walk up into clear blue skies.

Sunshine on the heights and cloud below, temperature inversion experienced on the classic traverse of the Five Sisters of Kintail, Nworth West Highlands of Scotland

13

Windchill

The combined cooling effect of air temperature and wind speed is known as windchill. It applies to exposed skin unprotected by windproofs and waterproofs. In any wind, but particularly winds up to 15mph, the chilling effect reduces the body heat to a much lower degree than the cooling produced by temperature alone. An air temperature of 5°C with a windspeed of 30mph gives an equivalent still air cooling effect on the body of –12°C (an effective difference of some 17°C).

Precipitation

Mountains attract precipitation. Depending on the temperature and the season, in Britain, the hillwalker can expect sleet, hail, snow, rain, or any combination thereof. Winds can then produce driving rain or blizzard conditions. If the ground temperature is below freezing – which is quite often the case – and it rains, the formation of verglas (see p.23) can make walking instantly treacherous.

Wind

Possibly the most influential factors in determining conditions on the hill are the strength and direction of the wind. Battling against the wind's force is an important consideration in the selection of any route through the hills. The pure physical strength required to walk against it is energy-sapping and tiring, whilst on exposed ridges its sudden force can easily blow anyone off balance with serious consequences. It can change the prevailing weather conditions extremely quickly as it carries with it clouds and their potential for precipitation.

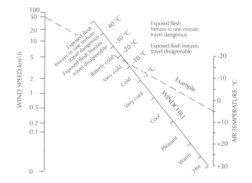

Diagram showing effect of wind and temperature

It is when the wind drives rain or snow that the hostility of the hills becomes most extreme, producing conditions where survival becomes a difficult and serious business. The risk of exposure as wind whisks away body heat and drives in the wet and damp should never be underestimated. But wind alone, even without precipitation, rapidly lowers body temperature and this effect is known as windchill.

Weather Forecast

It is vital that an up-to-date weather forecast is obtained before one ventures onto the hills. Radio or television weather forecasting is of a high standard, and satellite prediction extremely good in identifying general weather patterns. However, always remember that hills create their own individual weather. Some popular mountain areas have their own specific weather forecasting services and these should also be consulted. In the Lake District National Park, for example, daily weather notices are strategically placed at popular hill access points, and there is a recorded 'Fell Top' weather forecast available by direct telephone dialling.

To fully appreciate the prevailing hill conditions, knowledge of the recent weather history is important. In summer this will enable one to decide on the conditions underfoot, if soft or hard, or whether the streams, lakes and ponds will be swollen with floodwater. In winter, to read the snow conditions successfully and ascertain the many potential dangers, this knowledge is essential for safety. An absolute minimum of 24 hours should be allowed before anyone ventures onto the hill after heavy to moderate snowfall, and three days to a week is a much more practical proposition. (There is no fun to be had in floundering through unstable soft snow; in fact it is downright dangerous.)

Always be prepared for the worst and be able to read the weather signs to some degree yourself. This involves the ability to recognise basic cloud formations and have an awareness of 'weather lore'.

Weather 'Lore'

Hill weather can be fickle, with summit conditions unexpectedly severe, and it is essential to be weather-wise at all times. The art of reading the sky and the

Sky colour
The colour of the sky really is a useful warning and the old adage, 'Red sky in the morning shepherd's warning, red sky at night shepherd's delight', often holds true. Red sky in the morning is caused by the sun's light being refracted, or bent by moisture droplets, and a red sky in the evening is usually caused by haze (or pollution) and is a sign of fine weather, unless there is heavy cloud about. Other colours of the sky can also serve as impending weather signs: yellow skies predict rain and wind, as does an orange-tinted sky. Mauve, however, is generally only seen during a settled spell.

'Mackeral sky, mackeral sky, not long wet, not long dry' a northerly air stream blows in. Wansfell Pike above Troutbeck, the Lake District

A winter's morning with mist filling the valleys whilst the hills are gloriously clear and bathed in sunshine. An early start will pay dividends in these conditions. Looking over Little Langdale towards Ambleside and Lake Windermere, the Lake District

wind can be learned with practice and it is necessary to do so to keep one step ahead of the weather.

Likely sunshine can be predicted by observation of the clouds and the strength and direction of the wind:

- Small lambswool clouds with flat bases and rounded tops (particularly if they appear soon after dawn and move slowly) predict fine weather for a few hours

- Cloud particles that race in after a clear cold dawn usually mean showers before midday

- Shower clouds with billowing sides and cauliflower tops (developing cumulus clouds) should be carefully watched; if these further develop to present cliff-like formations with anvil-shaped tops (cumulonimbus) then thunder and hail is quite possible

- Thread-like high clouds arranged in waves or lines (altocumulus) normally indicate stable condition; however, if they become compact, showers can be expected.

There is a useful saying: 'Short notice, soon past; long notice, long last'. Sudden rain won't last for long but when sheets of cloud slowly build together, lower and darken, it will be wet for a protracted period of time. 'Long notice' can start also with tufts and plumes of high cloud that are replaced by a cloud sheet casting a halo round the sun, producing a 'frosted glass' effect prior to the sun disappearing. As the wind rises and changes direction the rain begins. A further saying is 'A curdle sky will not leave the earth long dry.' This is because the mid-layer of clouds in a dappled sky occurs during periods of unsettled weather.

Mists in the river valleys can often be left below when one takes to the hills. It is a sign of cooling night temperatures when the tops can give their clearest views. In winter snow can be predicted as the air becomes heavy and the sky clouds over during a cold spell.

In Britain, winds from the west most often produce rain conditions, whilst easterly winds bring the greatest extremes of temperature (both in winter and summer). There are other signs that are worth watching: increased humidity prior to rainfall will close the flowers of many plants and enhance such smells as arise from boggy ground or from the farmyard. Descending chimney smoke also warns of rain. 'Whirlwinds' of dust or soil warn again of rain and stronger winds.

The rules are: know the forecast and plan the day accordingly, but keep an eye on the weather and be prepared to change your plans if it threatens to deteriorate. The golden rule however (perhaps most appropriate for the Cuillin mountains on the Isle of Skye off north-west Scotland), is 'If you can see the hills it's going to rain – if you can't it's already raining!' In other words: 'Be prepared!'

Important physical features in summer: the hillwalker should be able to identify these important features and appreciate their significance.

a Trig point	g Deep, slow-flowing river	m Scree
b Arete	h Bog	n Boulder field
c Pass	i Lake	o Bracken, heather, scrub
d Hanging valley and lake	j Cliff	p Cairned footpath
e Waterfall	k Gully	q Coniferous forest
f Fast-flowing stream	l Rake	r Stone wall

IMPORTANT PHYSICAL FEATURES IN SUMMER

Trig Point (Triangulation Survey Point) or Summit Cairn (a)

This indicates the very top of a particular peak. The trig point is usually made with concrete and like the stone-built summit cairn can provide a useful windbreak. Neither damage nor add to these features.

Shoulder or Pass (c)

This feature lies saddle-like between two hills and often provides access between two valleys. Strictly speaking the bottom of the dip is known as the pass (bealach in Scotland, bwlch in Wales) and the gentle rise above, on each side, is known as the shoulder. Often the easiest and safest mountain approach is up a shoulder.

Arête Spur or Ridge (b)

These often lead up to or between mountain summits and in their extreme can be knife-edged. Typical examples in Britain are Striding Edge on Helvellyn in the Lake District and the Aonach Eagach ridge above Glencoe valley in Scotland.

Cairn (p)

Cairns often mark the safe path, changes in path direction or a route junction. They are often useful in poor visibility but cannot always be relied upon. Never build, or add to, cairns as they may destroy the wilderness for others.

Cliff (j)

Steep faces of rock should be avoided by the hillwalker and their position carefully noted.

Rake (l)

A rake is a diagonal fault line (geological break) across a cliff or hillside that sometimes provides a natural route. An example is Jack's Rake which provides an exposed scramble up and across the precipitous cliffs of Pavey Ark above the Langdale valley in the Lake District.

Gully (k)

A gully is a vertical rift in a hillside or through a cliff. It usually carries a stream and can be boulder-filled and/or stepped with large vertical drops or waterfalls. Whilst some gullies provide a suitable access point through steep ground many do not, and therefore pre-knowledge is necessary before attempting their ascent or descent. (Those carrying streams are known as ghylls or gills in the Lake District.)

Scree (m)

Steeply inclined fields of broken rock are known as scree. They come in all shapes and sizes and can occur below the summit and above or below cliffs. Care should always be taken never to dislodge rocks for one can never be completely sure that a climber, walker or animal will not be caught below (even if there is no sign of anyone, and no sound can be heard, this is no guarantee that all is clear).

Boulderfield (n)

Larger than scree, boulderfields can be very awkward and often dangerous to travel through. They tend to occur most frequently below cliffs at the bottom of scree.

Hanging Valley (d)

Formed by glacial action scooping out the side of a mountain, hanging valleys are variously named corrie (Scotland), cwms (Wales), combes (Lake District) or cirques. Often they have a small deep tarn (Lake District), llyn (Wales), or lochan (Scotland) at their bottom. There can be steep cliffs above and waterfalls into and out of hanging valleys.

Stream or River (f)

Even though fast-flowing streams may be shallow they can be extremely hazardous and difficult to cross, for the force of flowing water is deceptively powerful. During periods of spate (rain), or when swollen during the spring melt of snow and ice, even the humblest-looking stream can be lethal. It is also true that slow-flowing waters run deep. Careful inspection and selection of a crossing point is imperative for safety.

Bog (h)

Bog is saturated and therefore soft ground. Crossing it is never easy or pleasant, and can be dangerous. Beware of ground that rolls underfoot as this usually indicates only a surface crust of vegetation over water of unknown depth. If the crust is broken or gives way the consequences for the walker could be serious. This sort of ground provides a breeding ground for insects (midges and mosquitoes), as does any still water, and during the appropriate season this is another good reason for avoiding areas of bog.

See page 17 – Many hanging valleys (d) end in waterfalls (e) with no safe passage of descent. Great care should be exercised if the way ahead cannot be clearly seen. Taylorgill Force below Styhead Tarn, Borrowdale, the Lake District

Lake (i)

It can be a substantial hike to circumnavigate lakes (lochs in Scotland and llyns in Wales), especially if they are swollen with flood water. In some instances adjacent flooded lakes can join together and this possibility should be noted.

Coniferous Forest and Other Vegetation (q)

This can sometimes be almost impenetrable, with the spiky leaves and branches ripping both flesh and clothing. This can also apply to areas of scrub, brush and bracken (depending on the location and season) all of which may not be indicated on a map.

Wall or Boundary Fence (r)

Walls and fences should be treated with respect (unless they deliberately block a public right of way) because they all belong to someone and serve some purpose. Always use a gate if possible.

IMPORTANT PHYSICAL FEATURES IN WINTER

Winter transforms the hills making them into a very serious proposition for the hillwalker

Winter transforms the hills. Instantly recognisable summer features become completely transformed and the white snows cover all detail, producing aesthetically contoured terrain of remarkable similarity. Ice coats streams and lakes and subsequent snows hide them from view. When snow is on the move, drifted and

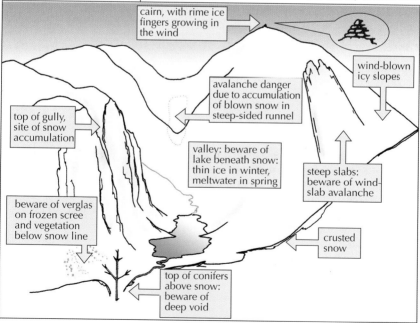

cairn, with rime ice fingers growing in the wind

wind-blown icy slopes

avalanche danger due to accumulation of blown snow in steep-sided runnel

top of gully, site of snow accumulation

valley: beware of lake beneath snow: thin ice in winter, meltwater in spring

steep slabs: beware of wind-slab avalanche

beware of verglas on frozen scree and vegetation below snow line

crusted snow

top of conifers above snow: beware of deep void

blown by the wind, it is as though the ground is shifting below your feet. Frames of reference alter and sense of direction becomes disorientated. Conditions can quickly become extreme with bitter cold and a complex system of hazards, making winter hillwalking an extremely serious proposition.

Snowcover

Never venture onto the hills whilst it is snowing or for a minimum period of 24 hours after heavy snowfall – preferably one should wait at least three days after snow before going up. Soft unconsolidated snow is not only hard work and unpleasant to walk through but also presents a number of dangers.

Blown Snow or Spindrift

Snow and strong wind produces blizzard conditions, and to be out in the hills in a true blizzard is a terrifying and dangerous experience. The white snow in the air and underneath the feet loses the walker in an insular world with no reference points. This condition is known as 'white-out'. Snow and extreme cold penetrate even the best of clothing and the walker is seriously threatened by exposure, hypothermia and frost bite.

Snow can be transported by the wind after it has actually stopped snowing. Extreme cold produces light, unconsolidated, fine-crystalled snow that is whipped up by the wind into clouds of spindrift. It is the deposit of unconsolidated blown snow and spindrift that produces one of the greatest avalanche dangers.

Cornice

Cornices, formed by blown snow, can occur along ridges and at the edges of plateaux or gullies. One should keep well back from any cornice as the extent of overhang cannot be seen from above and their break line lies well back from their apparent edge. A person's weight can break off or through a cornice. During times of thaw cornices are liable to collapse, so keep from under them.

Consolidated Snow

Depending on its age, and a number of different factors, consolidated snow can vary from being almost rock hard to sugary in consistency. Generally, depending on the surface hardness it is the most reliable snow on which to walk. Hard or ice-glazed snow (a wind-blown and exposed snow slope

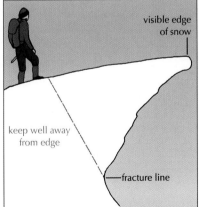

visible edge of snow

keep well away from edge

fracture line

Cornices are snow overhangs and one should keep well away from their edge

Cornice location: observe the continuous line of cornice along the rim of the summit plateau of Ben Nevis above the huge cliffs of its north face. From above, on the plateau, the cornices cannot be seen but the great danger of approaching too near the edge of the plateau is revealed in this photograph.

can be transformed into a field of ice) necessitates the use of ice axe and/or crampons.

Crusted Snow

Often with relatively fresh, unconsolidated snow, wind and/or frost freezes and hardens the surface crust but not the soft snow underneath. This is the most frustrating and difficult snow on which to walk, as at first it partially supports you and then collapses as you put more weight on your leading foot. Walking rhythm is destroyed as you sink deep in the soft snow below. This type of snow often produces windslab avalanche conditions (see below).

Raised Footsteps and Rime Ice Fingers

These are two important phenomena that can act as tell-tale signs indicating the location of blown snow and therefore the possible source of avalanche danger.

Anyone walking over soft snow will consolidate (compress) that snow beneath their feet. If the wind subsequently blows away the soft snow, the consolidated snow will remain in the form of a raised footstep. This indicates that somewhere below there will be an accumulation of soft snow and hence avalanche potential.

Rime ice is formed by the wind hitting a solid object; super-cooling of the water vapour in the air produces fingers that grow into the direction of the wind. Hence rime ice crystals, on raised footsteps for example, indicate the direction of the wind that has shifted the loose soft snow. Once the (forming) wind direction has been ascertained the likely areas of deposit in the gullies, basins and plains below can be established and hence, in turn, potential avalanche sites. Stay away from these accumulations of soft snow.

Avalanche Danger

An avalanche is defined as the dislocation of snow over a distance greater than 50m. This is a complex subject and avalanches occur for many reasons even on slopes as gentle as 30°. Everyone should be wary and particularly observe the following points:

- Soft unconsolidated snow and deposited blown snow is dangerous; watch for it at the heads of gullies or on slopes in the lee of the wind

- Layers of hailstones, subsequently buried by further snow, produce a likely failure plain, and if your steps punch through a top layer of snow to reveal ball-bearing-like hailstones (or hoarfrost) below then get off the slope

- Windslab, a firm crust over soft snow cut free by the action of walking or skiing, is a major cause of avalanche. If slabs of snow break away below your feet and slide down the slope then this is a sure sign of windslab avalanche conditions – get off the slope as quickly as possible

- Thawing of snow and ice results in cornice collapse and other forms of wet snow avalanche

Raised footsteps: these indicate that soft unconsolidates show has been blown away and therefore warns of potential avalance danger below. Observation of the rime ice crystals reveals the wind direction that raised the footsteps and therefore the likely site of deposit of the soft snow.

Frozen Lakes and Streams – Dead-Flat Plain of Snow

Beware of, and stay off, dead-flat plains of snow in the bottoms of valleys or in the basins of hanging valleys, as often this snow can cover and mask thin ice. Again one must be extremely cautious when crossing frozen lakes or streams. If not completely certain of the ice's thickness, this is dangerous in the extreme. If there is any doubt regarding the strength and consistency of ice then stay off it.

Verglas

Verglas is thin, almost transparent, ice. It can be formed when fallen rain is subsequently frozen or when mist freezes on the rocks and ground. Unless crampons are worn it can prove lethally slippery.

Frozen Weep, Scree or Ground

Often the hills in winter, without a covering of snow, look inviting and harmless. But beware if the ground is frozen – these conditions can be just as dangerous as walking over hard iced snow. Frozen weep water crossing paths can present a significant hazard for those not sufficiently equipped with crampons or ice axe. Frozen scree becomes rock hard and a slip, if you are inadequately equipped, can result in an unstoppable slide on steep frozen ground. That which was once soft grass and turf, with sure footing, becomes concrete hard and slippery – so don't be caught out in winter even if there is no apparent covering of snow.

Snow-Buried Conifers

Keep your distance if only the tops of fir trees are visible because it is possible that the snow will collapse around these; their branches prevent snow consolidation, with the result that you will fall down the void, which can be substantial!

ALTITUDE AND NATURE

Those who trek through high mountains – some popular Himalayan passes and Alpine peaks fall into this category – should be aware of altitude sickness and associated problems. Generally speaking one can experience real problems from around 4,000m upwards, but thinning of the air combined with lack of fitness and acclimatisation can result in altitude sickness much lower than this.

The physical nature and position of any walk in this sort of terrain should be carefully assessed:

- Is it high? Remember altitude means colder temperatures and in extreme circumstances brings further problems as described above

- Does it have steep rises?

- Is it technically difficult or potentially dangerous? Steep uphill and downhill climbing requires a lot of energy; make sure you are fit enough, and have the required technical proficiency to cope with the walk with a good margin of safety in reserve

- Is it exposed to the prevailing wind?

- Will it get the sunshine? Slopes facing north may never get the sun, especially in winter, and this may result in the walk being cold and unpleasant, perhaps with the ground frozen and treacherous

Altitude sickness
This condition results in nausea and headache. If this occurs you should descend immediately. Generally it will only be due to oxygen depletion and lack of acclimatisation; the symptoms will quickly disappear as you descend. If you have problems below 4000m do not worry unduly; as you stay amongst the mountains below this level, walking, getting fitter and gradually gaining height over a period of time they will disappear – you will acclimatise. Problems around 4,000m can be serious, resulting in oedema; so do not rush up to altitude without first acclimatising at lower levels, and if problems occur descend immediately.

- Remember that conditions will become more extreme the higher you get; there may be snow and ice or sudden storms. Are you prepared physically and equipped correctly?
- What is the going like underfoot? It may be hard and rough or soft and wet, or both, so be prepared and have suitable footwear
- How long is the walk? Have you allowed yourself sufficient time and do you have ample daylight?
- Are there suitable escape routes?

Walking in Lakeland

ORGANISATIONS REPRESENTING HILLWALKERS

In Britain National Park authorities provide a valuable source of information on all hill-related topics within their area, and local conservation issues are covered by a number of voluntary organisations. But more specifically the interests of hillwalkers (and climbers) are attended to by four main organisations:

- The Mountaineering Council of Scotland (MCS)
- The British Mountaineering Council (BMC)
- The Federation of Mountain Clubs of Ireland (covering Northern Ireland and Eire)
- The Ramblers' Association

The first three have very similar objectives. These include securing and maintaining unrestricted access to mountain land and supporting the conservation of the unspoiled qualities of the mountains and hills. They are frequently involved in access negotiations and will gladly listen to and advise upon any access problems that may arise in the hills. The Ramblers' Association is particularly active in dealing with rights of way issues, on a nationwide basis, and has much experience and information to offer the individual.

Details of organisations in Britain that supply access and conservation information and advice are given in the appendix.

THE HILL ENVIRONMENT – CONSERVATION AND ACCESS

The hills are very special wild places with a delicately balanced ecology. We walk these areas to enjoy their great beauty and sense of freedom. Yet we in doing so we are exerting great pressures and inflicting damage on this environment. If we, and future generations, are to continue to conserve the quality and uniqueness of our hills we must assume a high level of personal responsibility.

In Britain alone something like half a million people regularly take to the hills. The sheer volume of humanity produces immense erosion and conservation problems. Those that leave the paths start a process of denudation that is very difficult to reverse; once the protective mantle of vegetation is broken and the soft soils and substrata below are exposed, the natural processes of frost and rain rapidly complete the erosion process.

It is essential for the walker to watch each step, to tread wisely and keep considerately to the paths where necessary, and minimise footstep damage.

The Hillwalker's Code

To lessen our impact on the hills and conserve all that we value so highly it is necessary to adopt a certain standard of behaviour. This is not difficult and in no way limits our freedom or enjoyment. The basic principle is simply to be aware that your actions all affect the hill environment to some degree. The following code of conduct is a basic requirement and should be adopted by all hill users.

1   On reaching your chosen starting point you should park thoughtfully. Do not block tracks or gateways and think of others, including landowners and the rescue services, who may subsequently require to park or pass. Never take vehicles up onto or into the hills.

Accelerated erosion

At popular access points to the hills where walkers are most concentrated, evidence of this problem is all too apparent. Deep and extensive erosion scars trail multifariously up the hillsides. The old wilderness adage that one should take only photographs and leave only footprints should now be modified to: 'Take only photographs – leave and change nothing'.

2   Stone walls and fences are necessary to contain stock and should not be damaged. Use a gate or stile to cross, and always shut the gate behind you. If a wall is climbed and stones are dislodged these must be replaced and any damage repaired before you continue. Keep dogs under strict control and neither unduly disturb stock (cattle, sheep or fowl) nor allow them to escape. Do not walk through growing crops or sowed land.

Footpath erosion:
Footpath erosion, particularly at access points, is a severe problem and everyone should do their utmost to minimise footstep damage.

3   Avoid causing erosion as much as possible. Tread considerately without breaking the vegetation crust. Do not cut corners on paths that zigzag; keep to erosion control paths; and observe diversions where erosion control work is being implemented. Avoid running screes whenever possible.

4   Always take out what you take in and under no circumstances leave litter (don't bury – remove). Pick up and remove other people's litter. Politely but firmly rebuke others for leaving litter.

5   The effects of overnight stays should be minimised, and any stones moved to anchor a tent or form a protective wall should be replaced. Take care with fires (in many locations fires are totally unacceptable) and keep them small and contained. Do not cut down trees or break live branches for firewood. Pick a non-inflammable site in a location that will not be an eyesore or environmentally damaging – a dry stream bed, for example. Accidentally started fires can have disastrous and far-reaching effects with moorland and woodland being particularly vulnerable areas. During dry summer periods the fire risk is extremely high from flying sparks from a deliberately lit fire, discarded cigarettes and matches, camping stoves, and bottles and broken glass which magnify the sun's rays, producing spontaneous combustion.

6   Do not build or enlarge cairns or structures or remove natural materials – this destroys the wilderness. Take care that any water source, for drinking or cooking, is wholly potable and pollution-free. Take only from running clear water, watch for dead animal upstream, and never take water downstream of any signs of habitation or industry. In turn never pollute a water source; washing water should be poured away through the ground and not returned directly. Toilet waste should be suitably hidden and buried or covered with a stone.

7   Never throw, roll or dislodge stones – especially on steep hillsides.

8   Respect the flora and fauna. Never disturb nesting birds or finger their eggs. Never pick or uproot plants – preserve life, however humble.

9   Observe access agreements and restrictions. These may include short-term seasonal restrictions on valuable nesting sites or in areas that are used for deer stalking or game shooting. Individuals should

not take it upon themselves to break access agreements.

10 Be courteous and respectful to your fellow men, but strive to preserve the peace and solitude of the hills.

Hill Use

Whilst most will sympathise with the feeling that 'only God owns the hills', in Britain especially they are more than just a recreational playground and must serve a number of different functions. To allow this interactivity to work successfully and to preserve and conserve the environment it is necessary to have some organised system of management. Whilst here I will detail the system in Britain there are many basic similarities and shared concepts around the world. However, in Britain, the legal right of access to the hills and mountains is by no means automatic (see below).

Despite private land ownership the government has defined areas that they consider should fall under specific systems of management, designed to conserve and protect the environment of these unique and special areas. They include:

Protected and conserved by strict planning rules the beautiful Lake District National Park is Britain's most popular region for hill walking. Looking from Loughrigg Fell out over Lake Windermere, the Lake District

- National Parks
- Areas of Outstanding Natural Beauty (AONBs)
- Sites of Special Scientific Interest (SSSIs)
- National Nature Reserves (NNRs) (England and Wales)
- National Scenic Areas (NSAs) (Scotland)

Additionally there are two important independent bodies, the National Trust (England, Wales and Northern Ireland) and the National Trust for Scotland, whose aim is to own land to preserve its scenic qualities and natural history. There are also local organisations concerned with conservation; the Friends of the Lake District (FLD), for example, which ensures that the aims of the National Park designation are upheld in the Lake District.

National Parks

In England, Wales and Scotland these have been designated for the purpose of:

- Conserving and enhancing natural beauty and amenity
- Providing appropriate opportunities for outdoor recreation

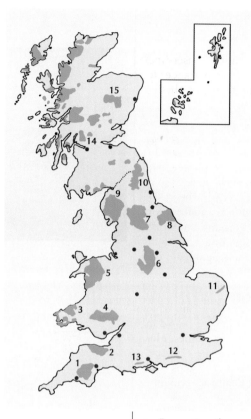

1 Dartmoor
2 Exmoor
3 Pembrokeshire Coast
4 Brecon Beacons
5 Snowdonia
6 Peak District
7 Yorkshire Dales
8 North York Moors
9 Lake District
10 Northumberland
11 The Broads
12 South Downs
13 New Forest
14 Loch Lomond & Trossachs
15 Cairngorms

National Parks of England, Wales and Scotland and National Scenic Areas of Scotland.

- Promoting the social and economic well-being of the local communities

These parks are administered by a National Park authority and each has its own plan which defines policies for all aspects of land use and management. All development is subject to prior planning approval. The park authority also takes an active part in the management: providing toilets, picnic areas, local transport services, interpretation services and a warden service to undertake necessary practical works, help with local difficulties and provide a direct link between the authority and the park user.

Areas of Outstanding Natural Beauty (AONBs)

AONBs are designated in England and Wales with the aim of conserving and enhancing natural beauty.

National Scenic Areas (NSAs)

These are areas of the Scottish countryside designated for their outstanding scenic qualities and in which development proposals which would have a significant effect on the environment are subject to special examination.

Sites of Special Scientific Interest (SSSIs)

SSSIs, defined as such by the Nature Conservancy Council, are areas of particular importance for conservation because of the flora, fauna, or physical or geological features they contain.

National Nature Reserves (NNRs)

These are nationally important SSSIs and are managed primarily for nature conservation.

Access

Despite the large areas of upland used by the walker in Britain there is comparatively little legal right of access. There are, however, designated routes the walker may legally follow.

Public Rights of Way

In England and Wales *public footpaths, bridleways* and *byways* all provide legal routes on which the public may pass. These are the responsibility of the county councils' highways departments, who hold the definitive rights of way maps for their counties. More usefully the rights of way are marked on the Ordnance Survey (OS) maps: Pathfinder and Leisure Maps (scale 2.5in to the mile), Landranger Maps (scale 1.25in to the mile) and Tourist Maps (scale 1in to the mile).

In England and Wales the Countryside and Rights of Way Act was passed in November 2000 and is now law. The current effects of this are still being negotiated through Local Access Forums and it will be a number of years before the extent of the intended 'Right to Roam' areas are defined. A similar act is being proposed for Scotland.

In Scotland the rights of way exist but there is no authority that fully records them all. The Scottish Rights of Way Society produces a guide to the law in Scotland.

Trespass

Legally one is trespassing if on privately owned land and not on a public right of way. It is *not* a criminal offence but a civil wrong. In England and Wales the landowner can take out a civil action against the trespasser only to recover nominal damages for the 'loss' suffered due to the trespass itself. In Scotland there is no penalty for the actual trespass and so a civil action can only be brought in the case of damage to

Long-distance footpaths
These now cover the whole of Britain, varying in length from 32 to 800km, and legal right of access has been successfully negotiated for all these routes (now nearing some 300 separate footpaths). *The Long-Distance Walker's Handbook* by Barbara Blatchford (published by A & C Black) details all these routes.

property. (An offer of a few coins at the time of trespass, as payment for any damage done, should ensure that any action brought will fail.)

Criminal trespass

Trespass on land owned by certain organisations is a criminal offence, and these include the Ministry of Defence and railway land. In cases of repeated trespass by an individual the owners can apply to the courts for an injunction (England and Wales) or an interdict (Scotland) to prevent this.

At the time of trespass a landowner, or his representative, who objects to a person's presence on his property can tell the trespasser to leave the land and indicate the direction for leaving. If the trespasser refuses to leave the landowner may use a reasonable amount of force to eject him.

If caught inadvertently trespassing be courteous and go willingly. Whilst you may not agree or understand the accuser's point of view do not lose your temper. It is much more useful to be calm and pleasant, but at the same time there is absolutely no need to be intimidated. By all means seek points of information (don't be too cheeky!) and know that if the landowner or his representative uses undue force – is physically violent, unleashes biting dogs or threatens or uses firearms – he may well be guilty of a criminal offence and should, accordingly, be reported for prosecution. Having said this there are times when the possession of a good pair of legs with the ability to use them is a decided advantage!

Access Agreements and Seasonal Restrictions

Seasonal restrictions to encourage successful bird breeding, or plant growth, or to allow shooting and stalking, are generally subject to careful and difficult negotiation by organisations representing the best overall interests of hillwalkers. Such restrictions should, then, be carefully observed by the individual. Other restrictions may include periodic closures for military purposes and emergency suspension of access in the case of fire risk or an outbreak of animal disease.

Private estates, even through they may be situated in National Parks or National Scenic Areas, are often used for shooting purposes (grouse and deer) at certain times of the year. During these periods the walker should stay away, if only for his own safety. The Peak District (northern England), for example, is divided into more than a dozen separate shooting moors and access can be withdrawn for up to 12 days between August and October. Advance publicity is given, and noticeboards carry the information.

Scotland and its many upland estates is famed, in certain quarters, for its stag shooting (red deer). Stalking and shooting of the stags usually starts in September and continues until mid-October. Anyone intending to walk at this particular time should check

their guidebook for information, or if in doubt telephone the head keeper of the particular estate. Although killing of the hinds continues for a longer period this, generally, does not pose any problems.

When fire risk reaches serious proportions in susceptible areas like moorland and woodland access agreements may be suspended, although this does not affect public rights of way. Signs and notices are posted at popular access points and one should comply with their instructions.

In Britain the Department for Environment, Food and Rural Affairs (DEFRA) has powers under the Animal Health Act 1981 to restrict or close access whether a legal right exists or not. Foot and mouth disease occurs infrequently and can lead to severely restricted access which, of course, should be carefully observed.

Black Sail Pass, the Lake District. This ancient packhorse route links Wasdale Head and Ennerdale. It is used by walkers to ascend Pillar Mountain or to visit the remote Black Sail Youth Hostel and was closed during the devastating 2001 Foot and Mouth outbreak

All Coire nam Beithach waterfalls above Glencoe, West Highlands of Scotland

EQUIPMENT

The essential prerequisites of hillwalking equipment are the ability to withstand the elements whilst otherwise performing satisfactorily, lightness, comfort and durability. Wise selection and correct co-ordination, complicated by the different demands of both summer and winter, require a sound knowledge of the available equipment and an understanding of its practical performance.

This chapter will cover all important equipment-related topics and individually itemise each main category. Suitability for summer and winter will be described as will correct care procedure, which is essential to ensure a full and productive equipment life.

It is generally true that you get what you pay for. It is a competitive market and if some products are substantially cheaper than the rest then this most probably means that they are made to lower standards using inferior materials. It is sound practice to purchase from a reputable outdoor leisure shop that will honestly help and advise. Select products manufactured by companies that have their good reputation and name to protect. In the hills you really cannot afford to have equipment that will let you down – too much is at stake.

FOOTWEAR

The single item of equipment that takes more punishment than any other is footwear. It is generally expected to serve equally well over mountain and through bog and go on doing so for some considerable length of time. It must provide the walker with sufficient comfort, continuing to keep the foot both warm and dry, over widely varying terrain. On steep rough ground it must provide sufficient grip, security and support whilst as the same time allowing one to skip along, unburdened, when the going is light and easy.

If the choice is made correctly you can purchase hillwalking footwear to give years of trouble-free walking. However, it must be appreciated that no one type of footwear can accommodate all the demands made by hillwalking throughout all the seasons of the year. Lightweight trainers, for example, can be ideal for dry summer walking, sometimes even over rugged mountain terrain, but are most certainly inadequate, if not dangerous, when the going is wet or in anything even remotely approaching winter conditions. However, some lightweight boots, correctly selected, are extremely comfortable, and can be used successfully in all conditions; but they are heavier and more cumbersome than trainers.

Trainers/Running Shoes or Walking Shoes: Whilst these come in many varieties they can generally be considered not to offer ankle support or protection. However, suitably selected, they are lightweight and offer good grip. It is important to obtain a snug fit.

The use of trainers can give you some of the most comfortable days on the hill. They are suitable for summer walking but will not keep the feet dry in anything approaching wet conditions and offer little or no insulation against the cold. The best have been developed for hill running and their main use is for short one-day walks where it is possible to change shoes, and dry the feet, immediately after the walk.

Trainers, as opposed to shoes designed specifically for hill running, often have a generous wedge of shock-absorbing material under the heel. This wedge is intended to take the shock out of road running where the surface is hard but flat. For hillwalking, over rough, uneven, ground, this must not be too thick. If it is, it lifts the foot too high; you will repeatedly turn the ankle over on hill terrain.

The walking shoe, usually leather, is a slightly stouter and smarter product. It is stiffer than the trainer with a heavier sole, and is more waterproof and better insulated. Because of this it is heavier, sacrificing some lightness for greater durability, and can be used throughout the seasons if conditions are not too extreme. Because the sole is stiffer and more substantial it offers 'edging ability' (where the edge of the sole bites into steep ground and supports the walker) which is an important consideration to those who wish to move over moderately wet or steep slippery ground.

Walking shoes

Walking Shoes summary: summer and even some mild winter use, but little resistance to wet conditions (water comes in over the top) and no ankle support.

Trainers/Running Shoes: suitable for dry summer walking even over rough terrain. Wet conditions will quickly soak the feet but this may be considered acceptable for short walks where a dry change is possible at the end. Inadequate insulating properties for cold conditions.

Lightweight Suede/Composite Boots: Made from modern materials these lightweight boots offer a high degree of comfort combined with some waterproofing qualities. They give ankle support but little toe stubbing or upper foot impact protection.

Insulation qualities are generally low and flexibility is high with little edging ability. These latter two deficiencies render them unsuitable for winter use if snow or ice is to be encountered.

Summary: A very comfortable and lightweight boot suitable for most walking needs excluding winter snow and ice requirements.

Lightweight Leather Boots: Made with leather and modern materials these boots are constructed using the latest technology. They come in various degrees of 'lightness' and one must select them according to intended use. Offering ankle support with good toe and upper-foot protection, and edging ability from the stiffness of the sole, they are generally suitable for all-year use over the roughest terrain. The stoutest of these boots at the upper end of the market are rigid enough to take crampons and are hence suitable for traversing snow and ice. Treated correctly (see 'Care' below) leather boots maintain a good level of water resistance and insulation.

When selecting leather boots one should note the quality of the leather for this determines the comfort and the life of the boot. Check that the construction employs the minimum number of seams, for seams offer a weakness through which water can enter. Examine the tongue to see whether it is sewn in and whether the lacing system gives an overlapping closures, again to provide maximum resistance to water penetration.

Summary: All-season footwear for rough terrain giving good protection, insulation and water resistance. Some provide enough rigidity for crampon use and therefore suitable for snow and ice.

Rubber and Plastic Shell Boots: Rubber boots provide excellent waterproofing qualities. They are eminently suitable for short boggy walks. However for longer walks they tend to be too sweaty and tend to rub sensitive areas of the foot/leg. Plastic boots (illustrated on the left) come in various forms. With the lighter versions it can be difficult to obtain a satisfactory fit. They are waterproof and remarkably durable and require no maintenance. The upper end of the spectrum, which is high-technology and very

Take note
Choosing the right equipment for the job is important, not just because of the expense involved, but because in extreme conditions, during winter, at altitude or in an emergency, your survival may well depend on it.

Lightweight boot unsuitable for winter walking or fitting crampons

Lightweight leather boots suitable for winter use and fitting crampons

37

expensive, provides the boot most favoured by the mountaineer and ice climber although, because of their rigidity, their suitability for walking over terrain other than snow and ice is limited.

Traditional Leather Mountaineering Boots: These tend to be heavy and difficult to 'break in' with the user suffering from blisters until the materials 'give' to the foot shape and become more supple. Their main use is over snow and ice with the use of crampons. They have fallen very much from favour with mountaineers since the advent of plastic shell boots.

There are some general points to consider before purchasing any type of footwear:

- Quality is extremely important; don't purchase poor quality products that will break down long before those that may cost a little more. Compare the cost of suitable footwear with that of a ruined weekend or holiday, or even injury.

- Comfort and fit are paramount. Each boot is made slightly differently, and each foot in the pair may vary in length or width. Make a great effort to select footwear that really is comfortable and actually does fit. Always try footwear on whilst wearing the type of sock that will be worn on the hills, leave it on for some while and walk around the shop. Always try on both boots – because one fits, it does not automatically follow that both will – and swop pairs if necessary.

- Be aware that, depending on the materials used, the footwear may deform or stretch. Some do and some don't; ask your reputable dealer about the

High performance plastic boots tend to be too rigid for comfortable walking and are designed for mountaineering and steep ice work

Traditional leather mountaineering boots are good for crampon work and climbing but are generally too heavy and rigid for comfortable walking

particular characteristics of the boot/shoe you are about to purchase, and then choose your size accordingly.

- Soles of all footwear should be designed to ensure grip. They must be of suitably moulded rubber that offers both wear properties and frictional grip. Soles made of plastic or other compounds are too slippery for hillwalking; even if cleated they will rapidly wear smooth, and their grip on wet rocks is comparable to that offered by wet ice.

Footwear Care and Maintenance

Use and Storage

Take care not to scuff leather or cut nylon (very easily done when contact is made with rock), and careful foot placement over stony ground is to be recommended. Storage of footwear should be sole down in a dry, cool environment, with nothing placed on top of it.

Drying

All types of footwear require the same kind of treatment (with the possible exception of the non-absorbent plastic boots). After one day is done and before the next, stuff boots with cheap, non-glossy newspaper, ideal for soaking up the moisture from within the leather or fabric. Remove the insole cushion, and tear and stuff the paper right to the end of the boot, and remove it early next morning. Additionally the boot should be air dried away from direct sources of heat; keep all boots at a prudent distance from fires, stoves or radiators. If composite boots are dried too quickly by a strong source of heat, the stitching is liable to break because of the differential rate of shrinkage of the different materials (nylon and suede).

Cleaning and Maintenance

Before drying the footwear, washing in pure water (a mountain stream, for example) or wiping on the grass in order to remove thick mud and dirt is sound practice. Otherwise (and probably the wisest cleaning method if the footwear is not soaked through) is to brush off the dirt after drying. In the case of suede/nylon composite footwear a soft copper wire brush can be used. For leather more vigorous methods, for example a very blunt dining knife (taking due care not to cut the leather), may have to be applied to remove hardened mud.

Waterproofing footwear
This is the most important aspect of footwear care, and should be done after the boots/trainers have been dried. Waterproofing is achieved by waxing and polishing in the case of leather, and silicone proofing in the case of suede/nylon composite footwear.

Leather

After each substantial wearing of leather footwear it is necessary to feed this natural product with a suitable wax. Firstly and very importantly, however, the leather should be sprayed with a silicone-based spray (G sport for example). Then apply the wax (G wax is based on natural beeswax), which is vital to maintain leather life and suppleness and to keep it waterproof.

Suede/Nylon Composite Construction

Trainers and lightweight walking boots also need to remain supple and waterproof in the outdoor environment. Silicone sprays (such as G sport) should maintain the appearance of suede yet give a high degree of water resistance.

Traditional Leather Boots

If after all this you find your feet are still getting wet it may well be that water is penetrating through the welt stitching. To test for this stand your boot (suitably weighted) half immersed in a bowl of water and observe, at hourly intervals, if leakage is occurring through the stitching. If it is, an answer to this is the application of Granger's welt seal. Alternatively use plastic freezer bags inside the boots, or Gortex socks.

If traditional thick leather boots are stored for some time in a dry atmosphere, without treatment or care, they will become stiff and rigid. The answer to this is to liberally apply neat's-foot oil (available from saddlers), wiping the outside with a rag and pouring a small quantity inside, swilling it around all surfaces until it is entirely absorbed by the leather. Stand for a while and the leather will regain its suppleness. This should be done very infrequently as an emergency treatment only, because over-application will make the leather too soft and the boot will lose its shape.

CLOTHING

To remain at the right temperature, comfortable and dry, yet have clothing that is light, flexible, and attractive, is asking a lot. However, with modern materials and correct application of the principles of layering, it is possible. Let's look at the varied demands that our clothing is expected to cope with.

Most hills require strenuous ascent, usually in the early stages of a walk; at this point the walker's energy output is high and he is generating a lot of heat. Later when the going is easier, or the body is at a standstill during a rest or food break, it is essential to keep warm.

Added to these internal variations, the external influence of the weather can swing wildly in a very short space of time: from hot sunshine to a bitingly cold wind, from fine to stinging rain, sleet or snow. It is easy to see that our well-being and even our survival depends to a large extent on how we dress in the hills.

Functional dress and selective co-ordination of clothing, then, must be carefully considered. Basically we can consider clothing to be divided into three functional layers:

1   The first layer which allows perspiration through but retains heat

2   The second skin which maintains warmth and weatherproofs under normal conditions

3   The outer weatherproof shell which should let perspiration and excess body heat escape, yet keep out the wind and precipitation

The First Layer

This heat-retaining layer can take on a different guise for summer and for winter. In summer, when the temperatures are high, it is important to travel light and cool with spare clothing – replacement first layer and second-skin clothing – in the rucksack.

First layer clothing in summer
Shorts and T-shirt or sweatshirt can be ideal for summer walking so long as spare clothing is carried in the rucksack. Above Wast Water at Hollow Stones, Scafell in the English Lake District.

First layer of clothing in winter – *in winter this clothing remains in situ:*

a) Illustrates a polyester-based balaclava-style hat. It is most often used in a bivouac and is usually kept in the rucksack.

b) and c) Illustrate polyester or polypropylene vest and long johns.

d) Illustrates short socks that may be used under woollen socks to soak up perspiration or as a spare pair.

In winter this layer most often stays in place with the garments, wicking away the perspiration to keep the body dry.

Second-skin clothing – *many combinations can be utilised to achieve the best protection for the prevailing conditions.*

a) Nylon tracksuit bottoms are light, flexible, comfortable, and reasonably hard wearing. They provide warmth and comfort and, combined with a long-john undergarment, are suitable for winter conditions. They dry quickly and are easy to wash and keep smart.

b) Breeches are a traditional garment popular on the hill. Often fabricated with wool (mixed with modern fibres such as nylon) they can be both warm and durable.

c) Long wool/nylon loop stitch socks offer both warmth and durability.

d) Light and easily changeable T-shirt-type cotton top.

e) A traditional shirt may be heavy and warm (wool) or lighter and cooler (cotton or nylon-based man-made fibres).

f) This is a fibre-pile type jacket with a wind and weather resistant outer shell. A zip allows a variable degree of ventilation. This light and warm garment can be easily carried in the rucksack when not in use.

g) This fibre-pile jacket is attractive and stylish but only offers minimum protection from wind penetration – an important consideration.

Second skin clothing – here we see a further choice; a co-ordinated combination of top and bottom fabricated from polycottons. Light and flexible polycottons are now a popular choice. Note that the water/wind-proof outer shell garment is being carried in the rucksack, as are a woollen hat and pair of gloves.

In winter the weatherproof shell remains in place – although the gaiters are shown above the overtrousers they would still be effective if worn underneath. Mittens or gloves are absolutely essential in winter; those illustrated here are fleece-lined nylon and it is usual to wear thin undergloves beneath.

The outer weatherproof shell – there is a large choice but the main

category of garments to be considered are coated nylons, breatable coated nylons and breathable laminates. Modern technology enables the wearer to stay reasonably comfortable whatever the prevailing conditions. If correctly selected, the garment will keep out the elements and allow perspiration to escape. Illustrated here are:

a) Coated nylon jacket. This, the simplest and cheapest option, offers lightness and a degree of water and weather protection. Some coated garments also offer breathability. The life of coated garments can be considerably shortened by careless folding or rough treatment.

b) This is a breathable laminate garment (Gortex) offering a high degree of water resistance and comfort. Look for strength and quality in the construction, weatherproof and conveniently sited pockets of adequate carrying capacity and cuffs (with velcro tape) that adequately seal the arm inlet. The hood, very important in extreme conditions, should allow sufficient movement, even when a woollen hat is worn underneath and should close sufficiently to allow full face protection. A rim in the hood is a great asset.

c) Overtrousers should match the jacket in performance. Look for adequate side zips which allow the overtrousers to be donned without having to remove the boots.

d) Gaiters form an effective barrier against mud, slush and snow, keeping the feet and leg dry.

e) Woolen hat or balaclava. Even if the jacket comes complete with the hood the warmth of a suitable hat is an important component of the outer shell.

First Layer Clothing

When the going is hot I personally tend to strip down to the bare minimum; even so, my shorts, T-shirt and socks usually end up soaking with perspiration. Along with my second-skin clothing, I carry a spare T-shirt, shorts or tracksuit bottoms in the rucksack, and change into the dry clothes if I begin to feel chilled. This may happen either if I stop or if the temperature changes (due to a gain in altitude or a wind beginning to blow, and so on). These items are so light that they can be stuffed into a very small space, and their additional weight is negligible.

The Second Skin

This second layer provides warmth with some degree of wind and weather protection. Chosen wisely it will be light yet warm, comfortably stylish but functional and durable. It should be varied and changed as conditions dictate, with spare clothing carried in the rucksack.

In summer and mild winter conditions, without undue precipitation and in the absence of moderate to strong winds, this is all that may be required to keep

In winter this layer most often stays in place with the materials, such as that illustrated, wicking away the perspiration to keep the body dry

warm. However, even in summer it is advisable to carry an outer-shell garment to guard against sudden rain or wind.

The Outer Shell

This is the all-important layer that protects against the mountain elements. You should choose according to your intended activities; at the lower end of the market (and the cheapest) are the coated nylons, and at the upper end the Gortex laminates of varying layers and

***The outer weatherproof shell**: there is a large choice but the main categories are coated nylons, breathable coated nylons and breathable laminates.*

plies. Chosen wisely the coated nylons can be perfectly adequate to resist a light or infrequent shower or moderate wind; they are very light and can be folded into a small space. The Gortex laminates and other breathable fabrics offer excellent weather protection in the harshest conditions, are light and flexible, yet are able to breathe, so that even strenuous walking is free from the soaking effects of perspiration.

Clothing Care and Maintenance

Generally it is important to remember that the man-made fibres have relatively low melting points and should be kept away from direct sources of heat. For example, gloves and socks that are not pure wool should be kept away from the log fire of your mountain refuge. Hillwalking garments can be grouped into four main categories:

All man-made fibres can easily be holed (melted) by sparks from an open fire. Do not use washing up liquid or detergent to clean them as they destroy waterproofing and also make it difficult to effectively reproof.

- Cotton/polycottons
- Coated nylons
- Breathable coated nylons
- Breathable laminates

All have their place in the market and budget, and function will decide which is best suited for your particular use. The care of these garments follows a few golden rules.

Use and Storage

All garments are subject to user movement, wear and contact with external objects. For the scrambler this may be the rock or ice brushing the garment, for the walker it will most probably be the snagging of trees or bracken. Correct selection of garment is vital. The traditional waxed cotton may not be breathable and it may be relatively heavy, but it is somewhat more robust than a proofed nylon – so choose wisely for your particular activity. It must also be said that all modern garments that are designed to be light, windproof and breathable are not fond of this type of contact and it should be avoided so far as is possible.

The life of a garment is directly proportional to its storage before use. If you look after your garment when not in use it will give you its maximum life before maintenance and further proofing are required. All garments appreciate being kept hung straight and free in a clean, cool and dry environment. If you crumple them in the bottom of your rucksack and leave them there, proofings will crack and flake, laminates peel and separate. So when not in use hang free if possible, and during transit (in rucksack or car boot) fold them gently and lay them neatly.

Drying

After use they most certainly will be wet from rain and water on the outside, and perspiration on the inside if they are not breathable; or even with water on the inside due to failure of the functional waterproofing system. All garments should be air dried, preferably outside by the sun and wind, and kept well away from direct sources of heat. Many waterproof garments are ruined (often with their intricate system of nylon fibres simply melted) by being placed too close to a fire or radiator.

Cleaning

Generally cleaning and waterproof systems just do not mix, and the rule is: if in doubt, do not clean. Breathable laminates, however, can benefit from correct cleaning procedures. Use only lukewarm water and bar soap (or flakes), and wash gently by hand. (Under no circumstances substitute liquid soaps or detergents for bar soap.) If you really feel that your waterpoof garment has to be cleaned, try light dry brushing as a first stage.

Maintenance

Even when all these rules are followed conscientiously, waterproof protection will beak down. Under these circumstances, or in the event of external damage, the life of the garment can be usefully extended by correct application of certain proofing products.

There are various applications depending on the type of material to be proofed. Silicone-based sprays (for example Granger's Fabsil for polycottons and coated nylons or Nylopruf for monofilament nylon) are suitable for woven fabrics. For light cottons and polycottons there are other products based on the total immersion principle where you hand rinse the garment in a solution (such as Super Pel). It is also now possible to obtain solutions to clean breathable laminates, and Superfab has been developed for treating problems in breathable coated nylons and with breathable laminates. Leaking seams can be sorted out with seam sealant (for example Granger's LP85 seam sealant).

RUCKSACKS

The rucksack (or sac, as it is most commonly called in mountaineering parlance) is an important and integral part of the walker's kit. It should be comfortable, with sufficient carrying capacity, and offer you the performance you require in terms of resistance to

Choosing a rucksack
Your decision must, of course, be based on intended usage, but remember the old adage, which I have found to be unfailingly true: 'The bigger the rucksack the more you carry.'

weather and equipment accessibility. Chosen wisely a good rucksack can last a lifetime.

Rucksacks vary from extremely light and simple kinds to those made from heavier, more weatherproof, materials and sporting ergonomic design, back padding, waist belt (really important if any significant load is going to be carried), compression straps to stabilise load and facilitate correct packing, outside pockets for ease of accessibility, external equipment loops, and so on.

Comfort

A rucksack should not only take all the equipment, clothing, food, flasks or water bottles you wish to carry, but should do so in comfort. On medium to long walks this is essential. Rucksack comfort is achieved through design with consideration for padding and style.

The carrying and waist straps should be adequately and easily adjustable. Achieving the correct personal fit is also important, bearing in mind the type of load you intend to carry.

Durability

Remember that although style and colour may look appealing there are many separate components that go into a well-made rucksack. There are a number of short cuts that can be taken, resulting in an inferior and less durable product, so go for a manufacturer with a good name and reputation. Examine the quality of construction at the most stressed and wear-prone points:

- Are the shoulder strap and rucksack body going to take repeated loading and is the strap itself sufficiently padded?

- Is the base of the rucksack, where it repeatedly makes contact with the abrasive ground when you stop for a break, sufficiently resilient?

- Is the back of the rucksack where it makes contact with you sufficiently comfortable, absorbent (cotton fabric is best here) and durable to resist a considerable amount of perspiration? Will the rucksack be comfortable if not stabilised with a waist belt?

Packing and Carrying

Comfort and ease of carrying is directly affected by the way you pack. Despite the presence of external pockets and gear loops, try to keep all major items inside the body. This stabilises the load over rough

Rucksack maintenance
Most good rucksacks require little aftercare, and the remarks made for clothing apply here too. However, over the years even the most resilient of rucksacks may show signs of wear and need some refurbishment – the best manufacturers offer this service for a nominal charge. Bear this in mind when purchasing.

uneven ground, and makes the carrying much easier and more comfortable. Use the compression straps to alter the volume of the rucksack if necessary. Pack tightly, and place the heaviest items at the bottom, ensuring that spare dry clothing and outer-shell garments are at the top ready to be extracted quickly. There is nothing like giving an uncomfortable rucksack a gentle kick up the back, after it has been packed, to smooth out those little undulations – but make sure your flask and camera are out of the way!

This group of equipment illustrates a variety of axes, crampons and boots that are suitable for winter hillwalking
a   ice axes suitable for hillwalking
b   eight point adjustable walking crampons (unsuitable for steep ground or technical climbing)
c   continuous nylon crampon straps
d   buckled strap

WINTER EQUIPMENT

Apart from the aspects of boots and clothing already discussed, those intent on winter walking should have certain additional items of equipment; namely an ice axe and crampons.

Be aware of the following points when you select your ice axe:

- The ice axe should be of sufficient length to be comfortably used, without unduly stooping, when walking.

- Make sure, though, that it is not too long; this will make it unwieldy when used for technical work, such as ice-axe braking, as described in Chapter 4. An adult of average height will probably find an axe with a shaft length of between 65 and 80cm most useful.

- A good axe will feel 'balanced' and should have all the important features (pick, adze and spike) as detailed in Chapter 4.

- Avoid axes that are designed for steep and technical ice climbing; they are too short and the pick is the wrong shape.

- Look for suitably strong construction. Your axe need not be heavy if made from modern materials. Axes can have wooden or metal shafts, and a rubber sleeve over the shaft greatly improves the grip on all-metal axes. They are available in a wide range of quality and price.

Crampons come in many shapes and forms, but simple easy-to-fit non-technical crampons (with eight points) are suitable for easy-angled hillwalking and may be all that you require. Most climbing-type crampons will also serve admirably for walking but they may be heavier, more sophisticated and too expensive for your particular needs. Ensure the crampons fit your boots perfectly (many types are easily adjustable to fit a variety of boots and sizes) and that you understand how to attach them – and can do it correctly – before you leave the shop. Generally if you do not have a rigid plastic boot your crampons should be articulated, in the middle, which allows them to flex along with your boot (if not they will tend to fall off as the boot bends).

The crampon attachment system must match both the boot and the particular type of crampons used. The traditional continuous tape strap and single buckle is adequate. Another simple but important point is to ensure that the single buckle of this fastening system is placed on the outside of each boot to prevent snagging by the opposite crampon points when you are walking. However better systems may now include a toe cradle and heel bar cradle or fastening. These are easier to put on and are generally more secure than the continuous strap system.

ANCILLARY EQUIPMENT

One of the great joys of hillwalking is its fundamental simplicity, and this means freedom of movement which is best appreciated when travelling with the minimum of accoutrements. However, there are certain items which should be carried in most circumstances.

Whilst it is not necessary to carry all this equipment all of the time, the map, compass, basic first aid kit and emergency food should be carried in the rucksack on most walks. The basic first aid kit is tiny, yet works wonders for blisters and cuts.

Many headtorches are remarkably light, and I recommend its addition in winter when the daylight hours are short. Check the batteries before each trip; remember that spare batteries will deteriorate even if left unused, and carry a spare bulb (usually this can be kept somewhere inside the torch).

Depending on the prevailing climate, a water bottle or flask is often essential to carry sufficient liquid to replace that lost by the body during the walk. A warm sugary drink, carried in a thermos flask, can work miracles in reviving a cold, tired walker. Equally, plenty of liquid in hot conditions is essential. Check that all containers have effective stoppers to prevent leaks. The all-metal type of flask is unbreakable, but if a glass-based flask is carried (which is somewhat lighter) care must be taken not to break it. It is wise to choose a water bottle that is of a size and neck design that will allow easy filling from small mountain streams – the wider the neck and the shorter the bottle the easier it is to fill.

NAVIGATION

Navigational skills are required to find one's intended destination by a safe route in any conditions. Practically navigation can be divided into three components which must be combined to some degree:

1   The ability to read a map and relate the information symbolically presented to the real hill environment – hence plot and follow a course.

2   The ability to use a compass to indicate direction and correctly orientate the map (whatever the visibility or severity of the prevailing conditions).

3   The ability to read the topography and correctly identify the physical world, to know the geological features and the flora and fauna of specific locations, to work out how the position of the sun can indicate direction and/or time, and to determine north from the stars.

The last technique is the one principally used in times past, and it is by far the most difficult. Because of the excellence of maps today, and the simplicity of using a compass, this last technique can get you into more trouble than it is worth. Although I will cover some of

Thick cloud below Sail in the north western Lake District

its more scientific aspects at the end of this chapter, you should forget about so-called 'sense of direction' and learn the basic map and compass work detailed here. On a rather embarrassing note, when relying on my mountain sense I have on more than one occasion been hauled back onto true course by some youngster in my party using map and compass.

The map is the product of detailed survey work (in Britain they are now produced very accurately from aerial photographs) and all the hard work has been done. Reading the map only requires familiarity and practice. Once the map makes sense the compass, simply by always pointing to magnetic north, gives us a constant reference point from which the map can be correctly aligned (particularly useful in poor visibility when no striking land features can be correctly identified) and allows us to follow along a determined course.

At the end of a long mountain day check the map carefully before night falls. The remote mountain sanctuary of Coire Mhic Fhearchair, Torridon Mountains, North West Highlands of Scotland

Before I enter into the details the following general points must be carefully noted and followed:

- In any party, do not allow one person alone to do the navigating. An accident or emergency may mean that someone else has to take over without warning.

- You should know where you are at all times and, even if you personally are not holding the map and compass all the time, share them at each rest stop or at regular intervals to ensure that you do.

- Taking time to look at the map to determine where you are and where you are going is fun; you will learn a lot about the surrounding environment and have a greater appreciation of your walk. Keeping in touch may well save your life.

- It's very important to keep in practice. In good conditions you may never need to use a compass; but think about finding yourself suddenly in poor visibility, perhaps in winter when snow is beginning to fall, and then having to attempt to navigate by compass when you are rusty. The cold will numb your fingers and your mind, unfamiliarity may induce panic, and potentially disastrous mistakes will be made.

- So remember: in good summer conditions, on familiar ground if necessary, practise the following map and compass work until it becomes second nature.

USING THE MAP

Map Layout

Maps are plans of a bird's-eye view of the ground, illustrating what you would see if you were looking directly down from the sky above. They are drawn to scale, that is, they are proportionally reduced in size from reality so that a large area of land can be put on a convenient size of 'paper'. Contour lines, drawn along equal heights above sea level, add the third dimension of height to the plan, illustrating the height

and form of the hills; on some maps hills are also made prominent by coloured shading, as are relatively flat fields (which appear coloured green). Other features – houses, trees, rivers and so on – are illustrated by coloured symbols, and their meaning is detailed as a key to each map. Importantly (in Britain) maps are overprinted with regularly spaced vertical and horizontal black lines (running north–south and east–west). These grid lines are situated 1 km apart, and are part of the National Grid.

The photograph opposite shows the actual view seen by the hillwalker, with the map below depicting the same scene.

Choice of Map

This is usually based on the suitability of the scale; too small a scale means that although the area covered by the map is fairly extensive, the detail is so small that many important features cannot be represented. If the scale is too large then the map will not cover a sufficient walking area. In Britain the Ordnance Survey

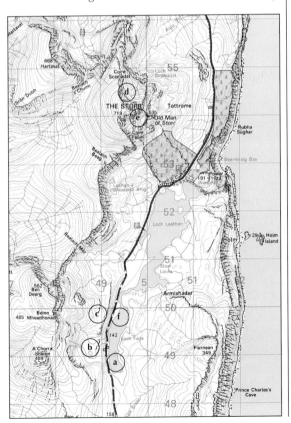

The photograph opposite looks across Loch Fada to Storr and the distinctive rock pinnacle of the Old Man. The map representation of the same scene is shown alongside and the common features are marked on both map and photograph, to illustrate how the real topography appears in map form.

a an island in Loch Fada

b the boathouse alongside the lock

c the road

d the summit of Storr Hill

e the rock pinnacle called The Old Man of Storr

f Loch Fada

Looking out across the tops of the remote Scottish Highlands reveals a complexity not obvious from below. It is esential to have practised map and compass work in good conditions and on familiar ground before tackling hill or wilderness walks crossing terrain such as this, for all such walks are a potentially serious proposition.

(OS) produce three different scale maps that are used by hillwalkers:

1. **Tourist Maps (OS T1–T11)** 1:63,360 scale, which (more sensibly) means that 1in on the map represents 1 mile on the ground, which since metrication converts to 1cm to 0.63km. These maps cover National Parks and popular areas of recreation. Whilst they can be used for walking (paths are generally marked) they were originally drawn up with the motorist in mind and carry, in the main, insufficient detail for hillwalking. Additionally they are only available for selected areas.

2. **Landranger Maps (OS L1–L204, which cover the whole of Britain in 204 maps)** 1:50,000 scale, which gives 1.25in to 1 mile, or 2cm to 1km. These are generally the most useful, covering both sufficient area and giving enough detail to travel the hills safely. Additionally they are comprehensive, mapping the entire area of Britain.

3. **Outdoor Leisure Maps (OS OD1–OD28)** 1:25,000 scale, 2.5in to the mile, or 4cm to 1km. These maps are purpose-drawn for the walker and the climber and cover only specialist areas. Although limited in the land area they represent (it takes four maps to cover the Lake District National Park), they are aimed at providing enough detail to satisfy the hillwalker.

The scale of a map is arguably the most important consideration, but there are others. Although the last two maps detailed above are beneficial from the scale point of view, they have other drawbacks. Whilst they are extremely accurate, produced by photogrammetry computer techniques, they often do not indicate all the features and paths that the older Tourist series shows. Additionally the Tourist maps are much more attractively shaded to highlight the hills and upland areas. The earlier maps were the product of land surveys where surveyors picked the information up directly from the ground and mapped it by hand, whereas the more modern technique is mainly technological. The choice is yours: scale and accuracy are obviously major factors, but detail and presentation should also be considered.

Map Symbols

Much detail and ground information is shown in the form of coloured symbols. A key to these is given on every map. Note particularly those representing rock features, making sure that you know the difference between the representation for the top and the base of a cliff. (Double-check on the map by reading the contour lines.)

The National Grid

Each Ordnance Survey map is overprinted with a network of north–south and east–west grid lines. These are 1km apart, so producing 1km squares on the map. From this grid we can:

* Determine distance
* Find the unique grid reference of any point
* Orientate the map by pointing the north–south grid lines along true north

Measuring Distance

Using the scale of a map it is also possible to accurately assess the horizontal distance of your journey simply by measuring. A ruler or the edge of a suitably calibrated compass base will do this, but to achieve a degree of accuracy it is necessary first to draw your intended route on the map. This will probably curve and weave round obstacles. Divide this route up into small straight lines of known length – the shorter the straights the more accurate the process. Then count the straights and calculate the distance. Alternatively, for the dextrous, a length of string can

Specialist maps
Special Orienteering Maps are generally too large in scale to be of use to hillwalkers, at 1:10,000, or 1cm to 100m, which cover too small an area. But some are now available for certain areas of interest and cover specific hills. Their most useful feature is the way they show the nature of the going underfoot, using symbols and coloured shading to indicate rocky ground, peat bog and so on.

The quickest way to assess distance at a glance is to count the number of grid squares separating the start and finish of your intended route. A route start crossing a square horizontally or vertically is, of course, 1km whereas a diagonal crossing is approximately 1.5km.

Direct route measurement from the map: this can be done by scale ruler – marking short straights along the route and add-ing the, laying a length of string over the route then measuring this, or using a calibrated map measuring wheel.

be placed over the route line and pinned correctly in place if necessary; the length of string required to cover the route is then measured by pulling it straight against a ruler.

The most accurate – and simple – method of measuring distance is to use a measuring wheel calibrated with different scales (available at most outdoor leisure shops), which is placed on the marked route at the beginning and pushed around. At the end it is picked off the map and the distance read directly. Do this three times and use the average distance.

Note that these methods of measuring horizontal distance do not take account of ascent and descent.

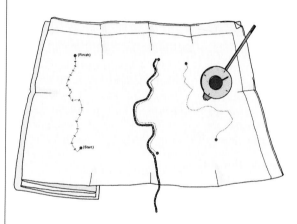

Grid Reference

On OS maps the whole of Britain is divided into 100km squares, which are given double-letter references (for example, squares SX and SW cover Devon and Cornwall). Each of these squares is divided to provide the 1km squares we see on our maps. Each 100km square is formed by grid lines which are uniquely numbered (1–99), and therefore a grid reference can be given very accurately for any location.

Setting the Map Relative to the Ground Features

In good visibility the map can be 'set' relative to the surrounding features. With your known position on the map as the central feature, turn the map until all the prominent features on the map correspond in relative

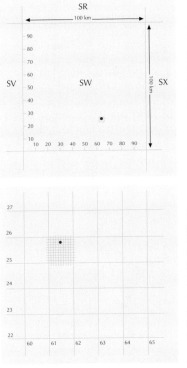

In Britain, each 100km square has its own double letter reference (stated in the map legend). This precedes the number reference

Each 100km square is divided by 99 north/south, and 99 east/west grid lines, that form the 1km squares. These are numbered from the south-west corner of the 100km square. Although only a part of any one 100km square will be shown on the map grid lines labelled, refer to the division of that 100km square.

Grid References:

On the map, 1km squares are labelled as shown here. To give a six-figure reference number these must be divided by ten more east/west, and ten more north/south lines. This is done either by eye, or by using the scale on a compass base-plate (Roman Scale).

The grid reference for the illustrated point is then 625/258.

The unique reference is SW625/258.

Note: eastings (north/south lines) are always read first.

Setting the map in relation to ground features

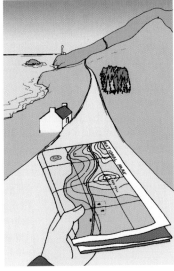

position to the actual features on the ground. In poor visibility, the map is set by compass – see over.

This orientation of the map allows one to follow a selected course easily. Keep the map aligned and you will be able firstly to anticipate and then to observe the actual land features as they occur on the chosen course. At first this may seem awkward; all the place names, for example, could be upside down. But think in terms of the representative symbols, which make sense viewed from any direction, as they actually represent the topography, and forget about the nomenclature. Using the map, thus set, is one of the most important principles of map navigation.

Use a map case
A transparent map case
hung around the neck,
with the map folded so
that it shows the area of
view, makes it easy to
check the route regularly
and keep the map set.
Anyone who has
attempted to set a map in
blustery conditions will
appreciate this simple but
effective refinement.

Contour Lines

These add the third dimension – height – to the map, and although simple in concept make the map into a very powerful navigational tool. Contours are lines connecting points of equal height plotted on the map at fixed altitudes, for example on the 1:50,000 OS Landranger maps contour lines are given every 10m, with a distinctively thicker contour line every 50m.

Studying the layout of the contour lines tells us many things. We can recognise hills and valleys, see their shape, and determine their nature. The closer the contour lines the steeper the slope, and its shape – straight grade or concave or convex – is easily observed.

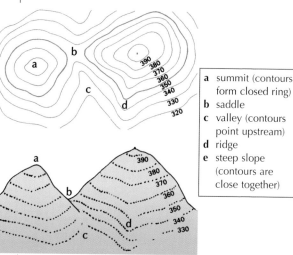

A 3-D sketch of two hills with contour lines drawn on its slopes and a contour map of the same two hills.

a summit (contours form closed ring)
b saddle
c valley (contours point upstream)
d ridge
e steep slope (contours are close together)

COMPASS WORK

The Romer scale
This is simply a scale, inscribed onto the clear plastic base plate of the compass, that serves to accurately divide the map grid squares into 10 equal gradations. Although a Romer scale is not essential, if a compass has this facility it can be used to accurately split the 1km grid square to give the third and sixth figures of a six-figure map reference.

All hillwalkers must possess and be able to use a compass. If you are lost, or if poor visibility descends, the compass is your lifeline to safety. Map and compass work is quite easy (although you must practise it in good conditions), and if you learn the following basic stages you will be able to navigate successfully in the practical situation.

The fundamental principle to grasp is that a free-swinging magnetic needle will always point to the north. This means that you have always got a constant point of reference – a true sense of direction. Firstly we should look at a modern hillwalker's compass to examine its many features. But don't be overawed by the refinements and additions: the fundamental and

The photographs show a modern compass, suitable for hillwalking, with transparent base.

a magnetic compass needle – north end red
b rotating compass housing
c orientation arrow (marked in base of housing
d direction of travel arrow
e clear plastic base plate
f graduated degrees – read against direction of travel arrow
g orientation lines in base of compass housing
h ruler scale for measuring map distance
i magnifying lens

most important feature is the simple one of pointing to magnetic north.

When using the compass keep it away from any metallic objects which may displace the needle from magnetic north. These can be on the ground nearby – such as a wire fence – or on you – for example, a penknife or metal belt buckle. In some areas, where the rocks bear the ore magnetite, a compass needle may well be severely deflected. In these localities use of a compass is not to be relied upon. The most notable area of magnetite deflection in Britain is amongst the Black Cuillin hills on the Isle of Skye.

Roughly Setting the Map with the Compass

With the compass at any known point it is easy to fix the true position of the map by just turning it around to align the north–south grid lines of the map with the north-pointing compass needle. You can now identify the features on the map with those on the ground and a visual bearing can be taken to your intended destination.

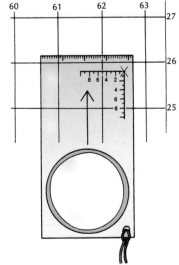

The Romer is used to measure accurate grid reference: here the grid reference is 625258

This is only roughly setting the map, because north as indicated by the compass differs by a small amount from north as shown by the grid lines. This difference is known as the magnetic variation and for all subsequent compass work it should be corrected for.

Magnetic Variation

To carry out accurate map and compass work it is necessary to apply a correction factor to the magnetic north indicated by the compass, because grid north shown on the map lies to the east of magnetic north in Britain. The map you are using will tell you what this magnetic variation is, for it alters with both your position and the year (the centre of magnetic attraction is actually moving slowly – the information is given on the map).

In the English Lake District magnetic variation was about 5 degrees – that is, magnetic north lies 5 degrees to the west of grid north as indicated on the map – in 1999 (reducing by approximately half a degree every four years).

To correct for this, when applying the compass to the map add 5 degrees to the compass needle reading (by turning the compass housing so that 5 degrees reads against the direction of travel arrow) to align the map and grid north correctly.

In Britain magnetic variation lies to the west (and its value depends on the locality); elsewhere in the world it may lie to the east; but its position and value will be given on the map, and the principle of correction is the same.

A further complication, which is mentioned for interest, is the fact that grid north is not *true* north (the actual position of the North Pole). True north lies slightly east of grid north, but it does not matter because all we are using is magnetic north – as indicated on the compass needle – and grid north – the vertical lines drawn on the map – with the correction factor given on the map that is the link between the two.

magnetic north
(direction in which
compass needle points

grid
north

B magnetic variation

In the English
Lake District the
magnetic variation
is 6°, as shown
here

magnetic north

6°

grid north

B

Magnetic variation:
in Britain magnetic north
lies west of grid north
therefore the compass
needle, pointing to
magnetic north, lies to the
west of grid north.

Navigating from a Bearing Lifted from the Map

This is the crux of all map and compass work. By aligning the direction of travel arrow on the map from your known position to an obvious feature along your intended route, you can read the bearing – that is, the angle between the direction of travel arrow and grid north – then simply follow this bearing using the compass alone. When you reach the obvious feature you take another bearing along the route to the next convenient feature, and so on along the selected route on the map.

Follow these simple steps to take a bearing from the map:

- Align the side of the compass base plate with your intended destination and your known position

- Check the direction of travel arrow is pointing in the right direction

- Turn the rotating compass housing so that the meridian lines on its transparent base are parallel to the north/south meridian lines on the map

- Remove the compass from the map

- Add the magnetic variation to the compass bearing (for example, for the Lake District in 2000 just add 5 degrees to the reading)

- Hold the entire compass horizontal in the flat of your hand until the red end of the floating magnetic needle steadies and points to north (N)

- Turn your body, keeping the compass reasonably level, until the red arrow and the meridian lines on the base of the circular transparent compass housing align with the floating red end of the magnetic needle

- To follow the correct bearing to your destination chosen on the map, walk in the direction of the direction of travel arrow

Although map reading is quite straightforward, it should be practised in good conditions until it becomes second nature. If you don't get it right in a howling blizzard you may never get another chance. Remember that the red end of the needle points North, and the red arrow in the base of the transparent housing should be turned to North on the map. Common mistakes are to align the red arrow/meridian lines on the base of the compass housing to the south on the map or, once the compass is removed from map, align it with the south end (white) of the compass needle.

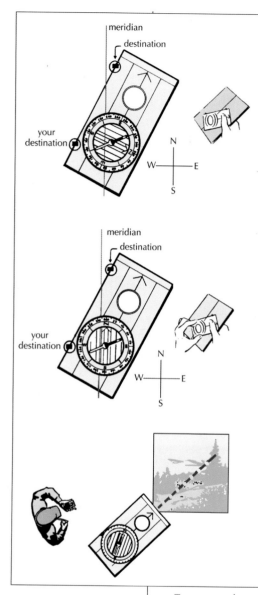

meridian
destination
your destination
N
W — E
S

meridian
destination
your destination
N
W — E
S

THE SILVA SYSTEM

1 COMPASS ON MAP

Place the compass on the map with the left hand edge along the desired line of travel.

2 COMPASS ON MAP

Turn dial until the compass median lines on the transparent bottom are parallel with the meridian lines of the map and North (N) points to the North on the map.

3 COMPASS REMOVED FROM MAP

Without changing the dial setting turn the entire compass horizontally until the red end of the magnetic needle points to North (N) and is parallel with the orienting lines.
Just follow the direction of travel arrow!

To prevent these errors always start by taking rough bearing from the map. To do this simply note where your intended destination lies in relation to your position. Is it between north or east (a bearing between zero or 90 degrees), or is between east or south (a bearing between 90 to 180 degrees), or is it between south or west (a bearing between 180 to 270 degrees), or is it between west and north (a bearing between 270 and 360 degrees)?

TRY IT HERE...

Take bearings **A – B**; **C – D**; **E – F**

(answers at left of map)

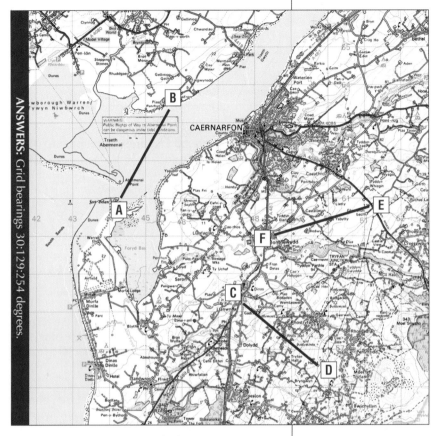

This is the essence of the most important navigational work in the field. With a little application and practice it will become second nature.

Aiming Off

This is a useful technique to safeguard against missing the intended destination. If the feature you are taking a bearing to has an easily recognisable linear feature running off on one side of it – say the straight edge of a pine forest to the left of a house – then it may pay to deliberately take a bearing (as above) to the edge of the forest. This is deliberately 'aiming off' and gives you a greater margin for error; once the forest edge has been found (and it does not require pinpoint accuracy to find it somewhere along its length), it is an easy matter to walk to the right and hence locate the house – the intended destination point.

Taking a Back Bearing

If you change your mind or wish to return to your starting point once you have begun on a bearing then you have to take a back bearing. Forget the complicated mathematics; just set the exact bearing you are following to the south (white) end of the magnetic compass needle by turning the whole compass so the orientation arrow aligns with it – the direction of travel arrow will now point along the correct back bearing.

Identifying Ground Features – Compass to Map

It may be desirable to take a compass bearing and convert it to a map bearing. Typically this is done to identify a particular distant peak in a range of mountains. The procedure is the reverse of that for lifting a bearing from the map:

- Point the direction of travel arrow at the feature

- Turn the housing until the orientation arrow aligns with the north (red) end of the compass needle

- Read the bearing at the position of the direction of travel arrow line

- Place the compass on the map, with the edge of the base plate through your known position and with the orientation arrow parallel to the north–south grid lines (ensuring this arrow is pointing to the north of the map)

- Subtract the magnetic variation from the bearing; with the compass needle and orientation arrow aligned, you will find that the edge of the base plate will point to the feature you wish to identify

Reading the map and navigating by compass constitute the most important and fundamental elements of navigation, and enable you to know where you are at all times. But if you do lose your way the following techniques may help. They are fine in theory, but some are difficult to use in practice and the importance of knowing where you are, at all times, cannot be overstated.

Finding Position when on a Linear Feature

If you have lost your exact position and wish to pinpoint it when, say, you are on a path or a ridge (a linear feature), first take a bearing to an identifiable feature, such as a distant peak, then subtract the magnetic variation. Place the compass on the map so that the lines in the housing (those parallel to the orientation arrow) are parallel to the north–south grid lines on the map with the orientation arrow pointing to the top of the map. Move the compass until one of the long base plate sides aligns with the feature to which you took a bearing. Continue this line from the base plate – your position is where it cuts your linear feature (the path or ridge). The technique is basically a repetition of the exercise of taking detail from compass to map as explained previously.

Finding Position from Remote Features

If one is in featureless terrain with only a general idea of position it is necessary to take at least two bearings to remote and known features. Repeat the above procedure plotting two lines along the base plate that, correctly orientated, pass through the known features. Where these lines intersect is approximately your position. Note that if three features are taken and three lines plotted they will not all intersect at one point (unless you are extremely accurate – or cheating!); your position will be somewhere in the centre of the triangle formed by these lines. This is known as resection and really requires a straight edge and pencil, for drawing the lines, to be accurate.

Slope

If one is descending it is possible to take a bearing directly down the slope. This is possible even in very poor visibility by getting someone to descend directly in front of you to the useful limit of your visibility – then take a bearing to them. Using this bearing with the compass-to-map procedure, if the compass is slid over the map so the direction of travel arrow (or the long edge of the compass base plate) is at right angles to the contour lines (representing your bearing directly down the slope), then this will be your position on the slope.

Rapid descents
Taking a bearing directly down a slope is very useful in determining the exact slope you are on, for example whilst descending a spur in poor visibility where it is important to descend quickly and you could easily take any of three different directions.

OTHER METHODS OF NAVIGATION

Whilst competent use of the map and compass is essential, total navigation relies on a combination of skills. Understanding your walking environment – the physical geography, geology and something of the flora and fauna – is an important aid to pinpointing your relative position. All this takes a degree of knowledge and observation that can only be gained with time, through both theoretical study and experience in the field.

Certain recognisable features are known as handrails; for example, a forestry break or mineral mine incline may be recognised as the quickest and easiest route to follow either to gain or lose altitude. Additionally types of vegetation can effectively fix an altitude envelope and may be a further aid in determining position. There is much more, but the best way to appreciate the signs presented by the natural world is:

- To be ready to learn
- To be observant
- To build your awareness by direct experience

Distance by Pacing and/or Timing

Much used by orienteers, these are two valuable techniques that supplement navigation by map and compass. If subjected to loss of visibility in a potentially hazardous position – typically on a summit plateau fringed by steep cliffs – being able to measure the distance you have walked from a known position can be a lifesaver. If you know the distance from your starting point and know the distance to your objective whilst following a bearing, or feature, you can pinpoint your intended destination with reasonable accuracy. An example would be walking from a summit trig

On the quartzite blocks of Liatach's Bidean Tolla'Mhuic, Torridon Hills, North West Scotland

point along the rim of the cliffs to fix the point at which the safe ridge descends (as when walking along from Helvellyn's trig point to the top of Swirral Edge).

Distance by Pacing

On reasonably level ground use the map to determine marker features 100m apart. Walk between the points and count the number of paces (strides) you take. Do it a number of times, work out an average and remember it. A typical average may be 65 paces per 100m. You can then work out your distance of travel. Firstly on the map, using the scale rule on the edge of your compass, measure the distance from location to the objective. Then work out how many paces you will take to reach it; for example, if the objective (the top of the ridge) is 200m away, it will take you (using the typical figure) 130 paces to reach it. So if you follow along the edge of the rim of cliffs (or follow a bearing) you can, by counting your paces, determine the point at which you have reached the head of the ridge and the safe point of descent. You have pinpointed the objective by measuring the distance, even though you may not be able to see it.

Distance by Timing

Another technique for measuring distance travelled is to time yourself over 100m travelling at your standard walking pace over average terrain. Using this figure as a base you can then calculate distance travelled and apply as above. Typical average rates of walking are 1.2min per horizontal 100m (12min per km) plus three-quarters of a minute for every 10m contour of ascent (see Naismith's Rule on page 73). At this rate it would take some 2.4min (144sec) to travel from the trig point to the head of the ridge some 200m distant, along a level plateau.

GPS Receivers

GPS stands for 'Global Positioning System', which involves 27 US-developed satellites orbiting the earth. A GPS receiver is a lightweight, easily transportable, hand-held piece of equipment that can determine any location on the planet using signals from these satellites. At the time of writing a GPS can pinpoint your position to within 5m. This is very useful in white-out conditions, over featureless terrain, or in a forest (providing you can get a signal and your battery power isn't too low). However, because of the complex

Take note
It should be carefully noted that each of these techniques – distance by pacing and distance by timing – must be individually calibrated and do not take into account stopping for rests.

terrain which hillwalking involves and current technical limitations, GPS can only serve as a useful supplement to map and compass navigation. Its most important use is locating your position when lost (and hence you can plot your route from the map), or as an aid to navigation when walking over terrain where maps are poor (true of many countries outside the UK).

Important Features & Considerations

A GPS must have an easily readable and clearly understandable display; a backlight is essential. It should feel good in the hand, be straightforward to use and have a good and reliable battery life.

Types of Receiver A GPS uses a certain number of channels to track the satellite signals. A 12-channel receiver is better than a 6-channel, and so on.

Map Datums Different countries/areas of land have different map systems or Map Datums. A GPS must be referenced to the relevant Map Datum. In Britain the GPS receiver must be set to OSGB or GRG36. The better GPSs have 100 Map Datums.

Coordinate Systems In Britain the grid of vertical and horizontal meridian/ lines (eastings and northings) enables you to pinpoint a location using a grid reference. However, the most common coordinate system worldwide is latitude/longitude (LAT/LON), used on the seas and in the air. This means that if you use a GPS in the Britain you must set the coordinate system to match the map – commonly referred to as OSGB, ord srvy GB, or British Grid.

Compass A practical hillwalking GPS should have a compass which works like a magnetic compass, that is, one that points to the required direction of travel. The excellent compact Garmin 'Etrex Summit' does have this facility and can be highly recommended for practical use. Unfortunately (at the time of writing) many GPSs do not, and are unable to tell you in which direction to travel until you actually start moving.

Waypoints These are the coordinates of a location. It is usual to be able to preprogramme in up to 100 waypoints for your planned route.

Built-in Maps Many GPSs can display a map on screen; however, at the moment these are only useful for navigating along major roads and are insufficiently detailed for use in the hills.

OTHER TECHNIQUES

Herewith some other techniques of navigation – interesting curiosities which may be of use at some time:

Fixing South Using your Watch and the Sun

This method is for GMT (Greenwich Mean Time) – for British Summer Time (April to October) bisect the angle between the hour hand and one o'clock. If wearing a digital watch there is no need to despair! The important thing is to know the time; then just split the watch face up into the conventional 12-hour face using your imagination (or a felt-tip pen) and carry out the exercise as above.

The Sun as a Clock

Knowing the time is important, and if you forget your watch the time of day can be worked out reasonably accurately by noting the position of the sun. Firstly one should know the time of sunrise and sunset and note the time of the year, then by reasoned observation of the sun's position in the sky the time can be told. Initially this must be practised when a watch is available to check out one's assessment, but sufficient experience and a little skill should allow one to tell the time to within half an hour.

Fixing True North by the Stars

To be honest this method is a bit dodgy; it is only applicable in the northern hemisphere, and can be easily foiled by atmospherics or incorrectly identifying the Plough (which is variously named the Great Bear and the Big Dipper). It is much better to get out your torch and use the map and compass!

Using an Altimeter

This additional navigational instrument indicates your height above sea level by measuring atmospheric pressure. It must be correctly calibrated from a known height above sea level and is only really useful in areas where map contour information is inadequate. A side benefit is its use as a barometer to measure pressure change if height remains constant; if the pressure drops overnight it would not be unreasonable to predict that the weather will deteriorate!

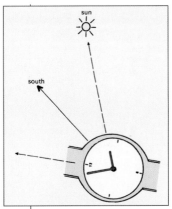

Fixing south using your watch and the sun: (for GMT) with the watch held horizontally point the hour hand at the sun and then bisect the angle between this and 12 o'clock to fix south.

Fixing true north by the stars: the two pointer stars are followd to reveal the position of the bright pole star.

Striding Edge leading to Helvellyn in winter, Lake District

TECHNIQUES

It has been suggested that there is little to say about walking technique other than that you simply put one foot in front of the other! However, to be safe and to enjoy the hills to the full, it is essential to know a good deal about them and about how you should tackle them. This chapter, based directly on hard-earned experience, explains something of that vital craft.

Firstly it should be appreciated that walking the hills is many different things to many different people. It can be a family occasion following a suitably mild route in the appropriate conditions, or a gruelling trek for the super-fit, in groups or alone. It can vary from a pleasant summer evening stroll through to a tough and demanding trip in winter. Whilst this huge variation must be appreciated, the fundamental principles remain the same.

Never lose sight of the simple fact that we walk for enjoyment. It is a way of getting out of the rat race into a world that is infinitely bigger than the perception of many city dwellers, a world where you are master of your own destiny. But it is a real world, and all aspects of hillcraft should be learned well.

ROUTE PLANNING – TIME AND DIFFICULTY

It is important to realise fully the scale and difficulty of your intended walk, relating this to your personal experience and fitness. Remember also that weather conditions make an immense difference to any walk, and, particularly in the hills, these can rapidly deteriorate. Route planning involves a pre-examination of the map along with an understanding of the information presented in a guidebook. From the map we can deduce much of the nature of the walk. The first basic technique is for assessing the likely time of the walk and is based on its length and on the degree of ascent involved.

Naismith's Rule

Proposed by the Scottish climber of the same name in 1892, this states that a reasonably fit hillwalker will average 3mph plus half an hour for every 1000ft of ascent (5km per hour plus half an hour for every 300m of ascent). Despite its many shortcomings (such as the fact that everyone walks at a different pace depending

Naismith's Rule
5km per hour plus half an hour for every 300m of ascent.

on their fitness, and the fact that the nature of the terrain affects each individual unequally) it does provide a worthwhile and reasonable estimate of the time you are likely to take.

Hence the first information to be extracted from the map is the total length of your walk (measured by one of the methods described in Chapter 3) and the total amount of ascent (and descent). Secondly you should also assess the difficulty of the route, and evaluate this in relation to your own (or your party's) strengths and weaknesses:

- What will the conditions underfoot be, bearing in mind the prevailing weather conditions?

- Large areas of rock scree or bog could make the walk much harder and more exhausting than a route of similar length, ascent and descent, but with easy going underfoot following a good path

- Are there going to be river crossings that may have to be detoured if swollen by flood?

- Are there escape routes that may be quickly taken to easier ground below?

- Is the route exposed, with severe drops and vertical cliffs below?

- Are there technical difficulties requiring use of both hands as well as feet?

Safety Factor

Safety factor
Your programmed destination arrival time must be a minimum of 25% of your total estimated route time before nightfall.

When all considerations are taken into account and you have made a reasoned assessment of route suitability and time, allow yourself a sufficient margin of error to finish your walk before nightfall. As a guide allow at least 25% of the estimated time of your walk as a factor of safety. For example, if you estimate your walk to take you eight hours, arrange to arrive at your destination not later than two hours before nightfall.

Whilst much can be taken from a map, guidebooks also provide a valuable source of information. Often this is summarised and requires some thought and interpretation to be fully appreciated. The following extract shows summarised route information for a walk in the Scottish Highlands, taken from a previous book of mine, *Classic Walks In Great Britain*.

The Walk: A mountain walk up through *the Lost* Valley to *the summit* of Bidean *nam* Bian (Glencoe, North-West Scotland).

Accommodation Base: Fort William

Maps: OS L41 – Ben Nevis, OL38 – Ben Nevis and Glencoe.

Start and Finish: The upper large pull-in, on *the south* side of *the* A82 Glencoe road *just* below *the* Allt-na-reigh cottages (map ref: NN 174566).

Length: 7miles (11km)

Approx Time: 7hrs

Ascent and Descent: 7,000ft (2,130m)

Difficulty: A high mountain walk requiring navigational competence and including some moderately difficult scrambling in descent.

Access: Car to Glencoe.

Seasons: May to October.

Observations: Superlative and contrasting mountain scenery with a huge vista from the summit. This mountain walk threads the easiest line through a wild mountainous region and is surrounded by large cliffs and precipitous slopes. Magnetite is present (particularly near the rocks of Stob Coire nan Lochan) and compass readings should be treated with caution. Good and settled weather essential.

Summit: Bidean nam Bian 3,773ft (1,150m).

A summarised route description: Much valuable information in planning a route can be gained from this brief assessment of the 'Bidean from the Lost Valley' walk in the Scottish Highlands.

The Walk: summarises and names the route.

Accommodation Base: it may take some time to reach your walk and this must be accounted for - don't start late.

Maps: despite guidebook information one should always carry the relevant map – safe navigation depends on it.

Start and Finish: car parking facility should be noted, you cannot always park *just* where *it is most* convenient for you, but *the* important information here is the unique grid reference.

Length: this is the plan distance, as seen from a bird's eye view, and takes no account of the actual slope distance.

Approx Time: remember to add the safety factor to this to arrive back at the starting point in good time before nightfall.

Ascent and Descent: this indicates *just* how strenuous and tiring the walk is going to be - because start and finish are the same point we can divide the figure in half and assume that there is 3,500 feet of ascent; applying Naismith's Rule we can then calculate the time of route to be 2.3 hours for distance and 1.5 hours for ascent, total 4.8 hours. Since the approximate time given here is 7 hours, we can assume that the walk is not a straightforward path and there must be some difficulty.

Difficulty: here is the assessment of that difficulty, it says it is a high mountain route which hints at exposure and states that there is some scrambling in descent which means that hands must be used as well as feet.

Access: some walks are not easily accessible and any particular restrictions, such as seasonal bans on access because of deer stalking, would be highlighted here; *Seasons:* although it is impossible to be absolutely specific here it is very important to have some appreciation of the route's suitability for summer walking; outside the months given here it would be reasonable (and likely) to encounter winter conditions which would turn the route into a mountaineering venture demanding all the advanced skills and equipment that this entails.

Get tough if necessary
If problems arise, do not, in reaction and without reason, seek help elsewhere. You may well be able to help yourself (or your party) most successfully from your own knowledge and resources. Do not always rely on equipment to solve all problems. Be prepared to think around a situation and modify your actions accordingly – a degree of mental toughness can work wonders.

Observations: here we get something of the flavour of the walk (I bet you wish you were setting off now) but also a warning that compass readings should be treated with caution due to the presence of magnetite in the rocks nearby, along with the warning that good settled weather is essential to tackle the walk. It is obvious that this walk is suitable for well-prepared and competent parties only.

Summit: many people like to 'tick off' the summits they have gained, in Scotland all summits above 3,000 feet are listed in the 'Munro Tables' and there is a great eagerness to climb all the hills listed.

When a route has been suitably planned, and it does not have to be an unduly lengthy or elaborate affair, all the above can be achieved with only a little time spent observing the map. It is necessary to be prepared for the chosen route.

PREPARATION

Knowing and being able to apply all the different sections of this manual, as and when circumstances dictate, is part of your walking preparation. But thorough and complete preparation is both a physical and mental process. The route you set your sights on and choose to undertake may have been selected for many reasons; whatever these are, ensure that it is within your (and your party's) ability under the conditions prevailing at that time. You must accurately assess the route, the weather, your fitness and your ability to finish it safely. This assessment is the first stage in the preparation.

Mental Attitude

Having the right mental attitude is probably the most important single factor in preparing for the hills. It must be fully appreciated that out there you are in effect on your own – even when you are in a group you must consider yourself, to a large degree, an independent and self-sufficient unit.

Planning is essential, but always be prepared to be flexible and adapt to circumstances. If it is logical to turn back; if the weather deteriorates; or if you or someone else in your party is unduly tired or perhaps suffering from sore feet (or whatever), then do so! Don't be afraid to make this decision, despite what others may say at a later date. You are the person on the ground, and you are the person best placed to decide on the correct course of action. Flexibility and understanding are hallmarks of good hillsmanship.

But there are times to be positive; times when you find the going tough but a cold logical assessment will tell that you are in no danger or real distress. Under these circumstances make the effort – 'Tighten the muscle, feel the strong blood flow' – for conquering that inner feeling of defeat will give the greatest satisfaction and joy at the end of the day. However, behind all adventure, excitement and challenge on the hills, let there always be solid reason and sound judgement.

Physical Fitness

You do not have to be an Olympic athlete to walk the hills; on the contrary, walking is a way to find fitness and health. Walking is probably the simplest and most effective therapy available to man. But take it easy and do it in stages. There is little point in flogging yourself to death up a mountain straight from the office desk

How far should you go?
You may ask the question, 'Just what limit should I be prepared to go to at my age and in my condition?' The answer simply depends on how you feel – age is hardly a barrier to walking performance and endurance. When I was nine I remember feeling great pride in reaching the summit of Ben Nevis, Britain's highest mountain, and running all the way down. I have a friend who spends almost every day covering some con- siderable distance walking our Lakeland Fells, and he has told me about the happiest day of his life, walking alone around the Tour du Mont Blanc (European Alps – 170km). He is over 70 years old!

when a much more enjoyable day could be spent on gentler slopes, where the air is still clean and nature just as resplendent. If you are out of condition or new to the hillwalking game just take it easy. As you do more you will feel better, and naturally more ambitious. Do what feels natural. Build up the difficulty and length of your planned routes gradually – enjoyment being the key to performance.

Essential Kit

Once the preparation has been taken thus far all one really requires is to get all the essential kit together. The wise have it all prepared and packed in the rucksack the night before, so there are no mistakes in the early morning light. Whilst travelling light and comparatively unburdened greatly enhances the pleasure, and makes good sense, it requires careful preparation to keep the weight down whilst carrying the essential items of kit. Whilst it is preferable if each individual is self-sufficient, one rucksack between two people is quite acceptable (particularly if you get the other person to carry it!).

The following items, presuming you are already wearing suitable footwear and adequate clothing, should be regarded as essential:

- Spare capacity and outer-shell clothing
- Map and compass (check it's the correct map!); a whistle is a sensible addition
- Energy and survival food (a flask of warm sweet tea or coffee becomes worth its weight in gold after a few hours' hard walking)
- Headtorch (essential in winter when daylight hours are short, and advisable in summer)
- Basic first aid kit (a few plasters weigh virtually nothing, but can save the day if the feet blister or if the skin is cut on sharp rock)
- Ice axe (and preferably crampons) are absolutely essential in winter, even if no snow is apparent. Hard slippery frozen ground and ice may be the order of the day on the heights

The above kit, if selected wisely, should weigh very little and correctly packed in your rucksack will be hardly noticeable. As a minimum it should ensure that your day is a suitably pleasant and comfortable one – and it can so easily provide the means to your successful survival.

FOOTCARE

The most important thing to you as a walker is the state of your feet. Sore or blistered feet can ruin your whole holiday, so don't neglect them. Having the right boots and socks is the first stage. Lightweight boots and trainers have made walking comfort the norm, and thankfully the days are gone when you had to carefully break in your traditional leather boots; a process that had to be repeated after each time they had been stored.

But feet must still be cared for – if you want to avoid blisters, take note of the following points:

- Only wear clean, comfortable socks, free from grit and grime

- Having a spare clean pair of socks to change into whilst on the route is well worthwhile

- At the first indication of possible blistering (if your skin is hot and sore), stop and cover the area with plaster. If you catch it before the blister forms, cover the area with a zinc-oxide tape that is sticky all one side. This gives the best holding power and protection

- If the blister has already formed, use the regular first aid tape with the antiseptic pad over the blister itself. With a little common sense, cutting to shape or carefully selecting the right size, and correct application, plasters will stick and remain in position. Ensure the area over which the sticky bit of the plaster is to be applied is clean, free from dirt, sweat, water or antiseptic cream (this is essential). When the plaster has been positioned repeatedly firm down the sticky area working with the fingers – the body heat from the fingers helps the adhesive to work

Another common footcare problem is odour – not to put too fine a point on it, some people's feet stink! There is no excuse for this. It is thoroughly antisocial, for whilst everyone's feet naturally perspire and smell accordingly this does not have to reach the intensity attained by some. If challenged the offenders often exclaim they are wearing clean socks, but one look at their trainer or boot may reveal something less than pretty.

Firstly the feet must be regularly washed and clean socks should preferably be worn daily – most people do this – but the root cause of the obnoxious smell is the footwear itself. The smell actually comes from the

activity of bacteria that have set up home in the boot – it can happen even to those who have the cleanest

Traversing from Great End with Great Gable behind, in the Lake District

feet. The answer to the smell is not just to clean your feet or wear clean socks, but to get rid of the bacteria *by treating the boot.* This means killing them off, and there are a number of proprietary powders and products that will achieve this with little effort or expense. Treat them regularly – please!

GROUPS, LEADERSHIP AND GOING SOLO

Walking in groups with a suitably qualified and experienced leader can be good fun. But never fully abdicate your responsibility. You must know where you are at all times (see Chapter 3), and know for sure that your leader is competent.

Leaders have full responsibility for the group at all times – on the hills this is something that should never be underestimated. If you propose to lead you should ask yourself two pertinent questions:

Consider others
A group can be rather daunting to other hill users; if you are part of a group, make sure that you remember your responsibility both to others and to the environment. Be courteous, let other walkers pass unhindered, and be thoughtful of just what you do and where you place your feet.

1   Why do I want to lead?

2   Am I fully competent to do so?

If you answer the first honestly, you will be able to assess your own motivations and so enable you to ask the next very big question. Leadership on the hills is an ultra-demanding and responsible task. Not only must you be thoroughly competent and be prepared to meet and deal with all eventualities in a way that inspires confidence in others, you must also have the qualities of leadership essential to keep the party both safe and satisfied. In Britain the Mountain Leadership Certificate is a minimum paper qualification for leadership on the hills. As worthy as this is – and I urge all aspirant leaders to follow this practical course because it is extremely good – it does not automatically give you the qualities of good leadership. These depend not only on sound knowledge and its competent application but on experience, maturity and certain inborn qualities.

Whilst it is most usual, and probably safest, to walk in a small group of friends, sometimes one will choose to go solo. Whilst you put yourself out on a limb with no help readily available should you suffer a mishap, it can be one of the most rewarding and challenging forms of walking the hills. The rules are obvious:

- Be competent
- Have definite plans
- Tell others your intentions, ensuring you leave a suitable message on your car windscreen as you set off (see Chapter 5)

It may sound trite, but it is true: I have never felt lonely whilst walking alone in the hills, but have often done so whilst visiting the city. The taste of this luxurious solitude, better than the finest of wines, is something with which you will not wish to part.

WALKING TECHNIQUES

Walking techniques must be suitably adapted to cope with the prevailing conditions and terrain, which in turn are radically affected by the seasons. In summer it involves dealing efficiently with scree and boulderfields, making stream and river crossings and dealing with other difficult types of terrain. When the going gets steep and exposed, notably in rocky places, progress may necessitate some technical work including deft footwork and use of the hands. This transition zone between walking and climbing is best classed as scrambling and will be given some considered coverage on p. 90.

If you choose to walk in a group, perhaps acting as leader, or walk the hills with family and children, you place yourself in a position of special responsibility and there are a number of considerations to be taken into account. Conversely, if you go alone certain aspects of technique warrant careful thought.

In winter under snow and ice the hills are absolutely transformed. They become a white wonderland of great beauty but can so easily become

During steep ascent break the grade by zigzagging

a cold harsh and unforgiving environment that singles out the weak and unprepared. Those who wish to venture into the hills in winter must learn, and practise until perfect, a number of advanced techniques including ice-axe breaking and crampon work. These are vital for your well-being and survival.

General Considerations

The important thing is to fall into a steady rhythm, one in which you feel comfortable and relaxed. When you find this natural pace your heart, lungs and muscles function at their maximum efficiency and you will achieve your best walking performance. Depending on the length and difficulty of your chosen route it is often better to keep going at an easy rate that suits you, than to take frequent rest stops. At the end of the day the difference between a pace that you find extremely demanding and one which is comfortable is surprisingly slight. The frequent rest stops necessitated by pushing ahead too quickly significantly increase the amount of time required to complete a walk.

When ascending or descending steep ground there are various points to consider to ease your passage:

- When making a steep ascent try to pace yourself – keep going at a reasonable rate rather than bursting heart and lungs in a dash for the top

- Avoid taking steep slopes directly, if possible, and use a system of zigzags to break the grade

- Be steady and maintain concentration in descent. Many twisted ankles occur here because the tired walker loses coordination allowing gravity to pull him along too quickly

- When moving quickly in descent balance is best maintained by adopting a forward-leaning posture, using the arms to counter any imbalance (windmill-like). Many tend to lean back, which shifts their weight into a position of instability and produces many a slip

- Take small steps even if they are executed rapidly – long strides taken downhill punish the body and lead to the risk of a broken leg

During rapid descent take small steps, lean forward, use the arms to counter-balance body movement

Endurance

Keeping going and making ground is sometimes an important requirement. Physical effort and the ability to work and keep working depend on mental concentration. Not every walk on every occasion is a continually unfolding delight with breathtaking views

Keep to the path

This may seem obvious, but is often forgotten by the inexperienced. Often the path may be vague – say a rough sheep track – but it should be stuck to wherever possible. Avoid the temptation to take short cuts, which often turn out to be anything but. A path will generally provide the best route and the easiest walking, even if it does not take the shortest route. Anyone who has ventured off a path into the deep heather, hidden boulder-fields, and extensive peat bog which abound in the average Scottish glen will fully sympathise with this particular recommendation.

round every corner. Sometimes, often with the advent of bad weather, a walk can turn into a pretty arduous affair.

In these circumstances it's important thing to think positively and keep going always with the intention of finishing – providing it is safe to do so. The key is to occupy your mind positively; don't think about the immediate pain or suffering your body is undergoing. You might think of your garden, your car, your family or the meaning of life, but underlying this must be the unequivocal belief that you are going to complete the route (which may of course be an escape route back to safety).

There are many proficient walkers who hardly notice the view. Their mind is fully occupied – the physical action of walking is but a means enabling them to think freely and undisturbed. Sometimes, in this state it is only the minutiae that are observed; eagles can soar overhead, the spoken word will be unheeded, but the colour of the stones beneath your feet or the intricate structure of the ice on the rocks will fill you with thoughts to ponder for many a mile.

Another useful technique to keep yourself, or others, going is that of target and reward:

- Set yourself an objective – a summit or definite feature some distance on.

- When you reach it reward yourself either by inward

Keeping to the path is generally the wisest course:
losing the path, or taking any apparent short cut, can result in many problems.

congratulation or, much better, with a piece of chocolate or some other 'treat'.

- Another technique when you are tired or flagging (but it is imperative to keep going) is to mentally divide the remaining distance into key sections of roughly the same length or difficulty.

- After one section is completed aim to complete the next, so dividing the task ahead into manageable 'chunks' of effort. Continue thus until the final destination is reached.

- Remember – have the will to endure and the body will respond.

The previously hard-working body, which has been generating a substantial amount of heat, is prone to a numbe of different sources of heat-loss when at rest. Don't wait until you start feeling cold. Take the appropriate action to prevent this heat-loss immiediately you stop.

Convection: even a gentle breeze removes body heat. Avoid wind chill , which dramatically reduces the effective temperature; seek shelter.

Heat is lost by radiation – eg. an uncovered head loses up to 50% of the heat it produces at 4°C. put on spare clothing as required. Remove sweat-dampened clothing and replace with dry.

Sit on rucksack for insulation conduction carries heat away through contact with cold objects.

Carrying Kit

Once your rucksack is packed correctly (see Chapter 2) the way you carry it is important to comfort, walking efficiency and safety. Pull in the compression straps to stabilise the load and neatly fasten back any excess length of strap – flapping straps can easily hit someone in the eye. If the sac is at all heavy lift it from the ground by bending the knees – don't lift with straight legs. Alternatively when you stop place it on a rock of convenient height so it does not have to be lifted when you resume.

With sac on back adjust the shoulder straps if necessary. On modern rucksacks this is done in situ by pulling the free ends of each strap, which are situated by your chest. The rucksack should be neither too high and tight on your shoulder nor too low and floppy down your back. When it feels at its best, the straps are correctly adjusted.

Repack if necessary
Once the rucksack is on your back it will be immediately apparent if the packing has been done correctly. If generally uncomfortable, or if anything digs into your back, take off the sac and sort this out. Sometimes a gentle kick works wonders; on other occasions you will have to repack your sac. Whatever the problem, take remedial action before you set out – an uncomfortable sac will just get worse, not better.

Always remember to fasten the waist belt to further stabilise the sac because this really does make a difference to walking efficiency and comfort. A waist strap also keeps the load from shifting, which is vital if traversing exposed ground where it is imperative to remain in balance. If on steep difficult ground, scramb-ling using both hands and feet (see p.90) never be tempted to remove the sac. When the rucksack is on your back your hands are free, and if the sac is correctly adjusted and stabilised it will be nicely balanced and will not impair your performance. Mountaineers on long mixed routes of considerable difficulty never remove their sacs – they just can't let go!

The basic requirements to achieve carrying comfort are the adjustable waist belt and adjustable shoulder straps – both should have buckles that adjust easily. The buckles should be sufficiently strong, preferably of moulded plastic, and be quick and easy to use whilst the rucksack is on the back. The sac on the left has elasticated compression straps designed to stabilise the load when it is only partially filled.

Rest Stops

If you feel that you need a rest stop then take one – the aim is to enjoy yourself, not compete in a marathon! But there are certain actions which are important when you stop:

- Your body has been working hard creating heat and losing energy. When you stop it is important to keep warm

- Remove any sweat-wet clothing and replace with dry clothing from your rucksack. Put on enough

The front view shows that each shoulder strap is correctly adjusted and the waist belt is tightened to suit. The rucksack should now immediately feel comfortable to wear.

This shows the correctly adjusted straps and the position of the rucksack on the back. Note how the back of the sac is curbed and padded to snugly fit the back profile. There are no long straps left to flap in the wind; they are all shortened or tied down as a sudden gust of wind can cause an unsecured strap to whip you in the eye or intrude into an otherwise carefully composed photograph.

spare capacity clothing to keep comfortably warm, and outer-shell (wind and weatherproof) garments as required

- Insulate yourself from the cold ground, particularly from rock, by sitting on your rucksack if necessary
- Pick a sheltered rest stop out of the wind – wind is the greatest source of heat loss
- Now you are relaxing it is a very good time to replace some of that energy you have lost, and to enjoy some food and preferably a hot drink

Hard Rough Ground

Rough ground takes many forms, but the common feature is that it makes going difficult. The feet suffer the most and over stony ground or chalk with flints, the toe and ankle protection offered by a good pair of boots will be appreciated. Careful footwork is necessary and, especially if there is a long way to go, one should place the feet as carefully as possible.

Scree and Boulderfields

***Try to avoid
ascending scree***
Try to avoid ascending or
crossing scree. Going
directly up scree is often
the classic walker's
nightmare of one step
forward and two back. If it
is unavoidable try to find
larger rocks that will not
roll so readily and step
only on these. If crossing,
look for a sheep or wild
animal tracks where the
scree will be consolidated
sufficiently to bear your
weight if reasonable care
is taken.

Scree can be either a problem or great fun depending
on your direction of travel. Descending scree can be
done extremely quickly by scree running. The scree
must be suitably finely sized and flow down the
hillside unhindered by boulders or rocks that are too
large to roll. Simply run down the scree, going with
the flow, using much the same technique as one would
if skiing. Lean forward, jump and swerve: it's athletic
and enjoyable.

Boulderfields are a jumbled collection of large
rocks often found at the base of scree. They can make
the going difficult, tiring and quite often dangerous.
Just because a boulder is impressively sized does not
necessarily mean that it is stable. Remember the
adage: 'The bigger they are the harder they fall'. Often
it will be found that a collection of boulders is
precariously keyed together and that if one is disturbed
all begin to move. Often also, the small holes at foot
level are not only deep but widen out, cavern like,
below and a watchful eye must be kept so as not to fall
down one of these.

Scree running is great fun:
*lean forward, go with the
flow, jump and swerve*

If a foot is caught down a hole, or a rock moves to trap an ankle or leg, take note of the following:

- Keep calm. Don't pull blindly and tug wildly; this is more likely to injure you than anything else

- Assess the position and attempt to squeeze gently out, shifting and turning the trapped limb to try different angles

- If your foot is down a hole that has not been subject to any rock movement, you will be able to extract it when you find the angle at which it entered the hole

- However, if the rocks have moved and so trapped the foot each situation will be different and will require very careful analysis. Depending on the stability of the whole mass it may be appropriate to apply the principle of levers where a suitably sized stick (or sticks) is used to lever up and lift the entrapping rocks (see Chapter 5, p.121).

Vegetation

Most hardier forms of vegetation present problems in varying degrees. Heather looks innocuous enough, but in its most luxuriant and wild state can be extremely tiring to walk over. Even the humble fern, bracken, can grow in Britain to head height and is exhausting to penetrate. Take care too, because when pulled in the hands the stems crush to form stringy laminates that are as sharp as any razor.

Those of us who have made the mistake of attempting to cut through a close-planted pine forest know all about the problems of this particular feature; ripped flesh, spiked eyes and kit covered in glutinous resin are just some. Each part of the world has its own particular delights in vegetation and for all, the message is the same: *avoid dense areas of vegetation* whenever possible. If it can't be avoided, be ready for the special problems you will encounter and make due allowance in the timing of your overall programme.

Using a Stick

Correctly used, a stick can be a considerable asset in the hills. Used as a third leg it maintains balance in much the same fashion as a ski pole, allowing the arm and flexion of the upper body to relieve some of the load on the legs. It is also of considerable benefit when you stop and rest. A contemplation of the view or a few minutes' breather can be taken quite happily whilst leaning with both hands on the stick.

The adjustable telescopic walking pole illustrated here is well-suited for the modern hill walker.

The stick must suit you height, be light and strong yet have a degree of flexibility to prevent breakage. its head should be sufficiently 'grippable' and its base should have a steel ferrule. Traditional woods include hazel and cane.

This hill walker has been assisted by the use of two walking poles whilst ascending this steep rock slab, and the boulder field below. Successful use of two poles takes a little time to master but once the skill has been learnt there are considerable benefits. The Great Slab, Bowfell, Great Langdale, the Lake District

What is scrambling?
Scrambling happens when you leave the beaten track or path and tackle steeper more challenging and altogether more exciting ground. It isn't quite climbing and generally doesn't require the use of rope or cumbersome equipment, but does require use of both hands and feet. It may tackle an irresistible slab of rough volcanic rock shining in the sun, a deep gully complete with waterfalls and rock pools, a natural rake leading safely across a steep crag, or a natural ridge of rock and heather climbing skywards to some distant mountain top.

The stick is also useful to test uncertain ground, for example potentially bottomless bogs or rivers of unknown depth. I'm sure one can imagine many other uses, but suffice it to say that hill folk of all countries have used the humble stick in their daily work for generations.

A suitable walking stick must be light and strong, yet must flex to a degree to absorb shock and prevent breakage. The head (handle) must be suitably 'grippable' yet neither too heavy nor too clumsy. Traditional 'sticks' are made from either hazel or cane and must have a metal ferrule base to prevent wear and splitting of the wood. Size is another important consideration, and you must select the stick to suit you.

Walking Poles

Lightweight alloy telescopic walking poles are justifiably very popular on the hills today. They compress easily and can be quickly placed in the rucksack should they get in the way. They may be used singly, leaving one hand free, or in pairs. Their use activates the upper body muscles and considerably reduces the loading on leg muscles, knees and feet. It is reckoned that two poles used in descent reduces the shock loading to the knees by some 40%. A huge factor when carrying a heavy rucksack. The mode of use will be varied with the terrain, though it is normal either to place the leading pole opposite to the leading foot or same pole with same leading foot. Using two poles takes a little practice, but it is worth persevering to get the technique so it becomes second nature.

Scrambling

Scrambling offers even the accomplished hillwalker another dimension. It's free from the restraint of path and waymark, outside the straight and narrow and requires a spirit for adventure.

Scrambling is open to everyone, and there is a wide range of difficulty. I'm going to define four grades of difficulty. These encompass everything from rough ground with a short rocky step or two to high mountain challenges such as Jack's Rake on Pavey Ark, Pinnacle Ridge on St Sunday Crag, Broad Stand on Scafell and the Aonach Eagach Ridge above Glencoe (the latter three all lying within the Grade 3 category).

Difficulty

For summer conditions these will be expressed in Scrambling Grade from 1 to 4:

Remember...

Take note of these two important rules when scrambling:

1. *Keep calm* – if you are going to fall then you will anyway, so there really is no point in worrying

2. *Maintain three points of contact* – which logically actually makes the technique more secure than walking

- *Summer Grade 1* is a straightforward scramble (use of hands as well as feet required) with little route-finding difficulty. The described route takes the most interesting line, which can usually be varied or avoided. Generally exposure is not great, though care must always be exercised to avoid a slip

- *Summer Grade 2* contains longer and more difficult sections of scrambling. A rope may be useful for safety on particularly exposed places.

91

Some skill in route finding is necessary, and some sections may be inescapable.

- *Summer Grade 3* is a serious undertaking only to be attempted by those with proven basic climbing and ropework skills. A rope may be advisable for safety on exposed sections, and it may be necessary to abseil or be able to scale pitches of technically easy rock climbing.

- *Summer Grade 4* is the hardest category, only really suitable for rock-climbers having a day off! Whilst the technical difficulties may be akin to those of a simple rock climb, overall, taking into account the combined factors of exposure, danger and length, they fall just short of a true gradeable rock climb.

Occasionally in winter a route can be ascended when under snow and ice. In these conditions a scramble becomes elevated to a winter mountaineering climb. Competent use of ice axe and crampons are essential and a separate system of grading the difficulty will be used. When under snow and ice a Winter Mountaineering Grade from I to III applies:

- *Winter Grade I* represents easy angled ridges or snow gullies around around 45 degrees. Cornices may be encountered.

- *Winter Grade II* is where steep snow or short ice pitches may be encountered and more difficult and involved ridges (usually classed as a summer Scrambling Grade I upwards).

- *Winter Grade III* is where difficulties are more sustained than in Grade II, and there may be significant ice pitches or technical ridge or buttress sections.

Techniques and Equipment

Good footwear is probably the most important single item of equipment. Lightweight boots or suitable trainers should be of good fit, offer good edge and toe support, and be of a high friction rubber. Note that some boots and trainers which offer acceptable sticking power in the dry can become lethally slippery in wet conditions. Having a boot that retains good frictional qualities in wet conditions is essential. On the harder scrambles a knowledge and ability of simple ropework and climbing safety equipment and techniques are important. This involves rope, slings, karabiners and helmet, with a working knowledge of how to belay and place runners for protection.

Most walkers are capable of dealing with a mild scramble no matter how wary of heights or weakness of arm. Indeed many children will walk an exposed ridge or bound up a rock bluff without so much as a second thought. Take things in easy stages, make the initial step and proceed at your own pace. Keep calm under all circumstances. If you get an overwhelming feeling that you are about to fall just breathe deeply and relax. Remember the classic rule of mountaineering and always maintain three points of contact: either two feet and a hand on the rock or two hands and a foot – knees and elbows don't count. This means if you think positively about it you are pretty secure, for in normal walking you have only two points of contact.

Crossing Bog or Swampy Ground

If at all possible avoid this kind of terrain. It is very easy to find yourself in much softer and wetter ground than was first apparent. Bogs and swamps occur in areas where water drainage is restricted. In its mildest form the ground and covering vegetation is simply saturated, the ground becomes soft and, predictably, you sink. But even here the suction effect which makes it an effort to remove your boot will be apparent. However, with a little effort it will be possible to remove one foot after the other until firm ground is reached.

The next form occurs when the volume and head of water builds up. The ground itself will begin to 'float' and become fluid. In effect you are now stepping into something that is bottomless – and you have got real problems. This is the principle of the 'sinking sands' that regularly occur in estuarine environments. Contrary to popular belief you will not be sucked down; the suction effect only occurs when you lift yourself out from the fluid mass/swamp. When you pull yourself out you create a void or vacuum beneath you which then pulls you back – given time, the vacuum will be filled with the slow-moving viscous fluid you are in, or with air when it can get into the void.

When in a bog...
The first reaction is generally one of amusement; of being stuck in the mud, which looks harmless, is strange and immediately feels rather silly. The second reaction is usually one of extreme panic and you thrash wildly about. This must be avoided: it burns energy fast and causes you to sink more quickly; you should keep calm, move slowly but act quickly.

Feet stuck: often in soft ground, it is possible, with effort, to life one foot out and then the other. Remove the leading foot and place behind on firm ground

It is possible to extricate yourself by following the correct technique, which involves the principle of spreading the load:

A

It is always possible to extricate yourself from a bog so long as you keep calm and adopt the principle of spreading your load.
A. Feet and legs stuck: take off jacket, jumper or rucksack and place it behind you. Flop backwards, spreading the load, then slowing remove legs from the bog.
B. Stuck up to torso and above: take off top or rucksack if possible and spread in front, then adopt the above procedure. If top cannot be removed, then lie forward and adopt a swimming technique.

- If you are in a party and your companions come to assist you ensure that they are not going to be similarly trapped; they must be on suitably firm ground.
- The first things to sink will be your feet and legs. At this stage when your arms and upper body are free remove your jacket or top, and spread it onto the ground over as wide an area as possible. If you know that the ground in the direction you have come from is firm, spread the jacket behind you.
- Flop over down onto the jacket, spreading your weight out across it. Make an effort to pull out those trapped legs and feet.
- Carefully retrace your steps – do not stop. Keep those feet moving, gently and surely but moving. A log or any other nearby object can be used to spread the load. If anyone else in your party cannot safely get near to you they can help by throwing these within your reach.

B

If you find that you have sunk up to the torso, adopt the following procedure:
- Attempt to get your jacket off and spread your weight onto it
- If this can't be done, don't panic. It is still possible to get out – your body has its own natural buoyancy
- Lie fully in the bog, getting your body as horizontal as possible and then use your arms in a swimming motion

- It will take time, but you can in effect swim out of this situation. Your body will be relatively more buoyant here (it is actually easier to float in a bog than in water), but the fluid is somewhat more viscous and horizontal movement will require greater effort.

It is possible to walk across other types of bog and feel the ground roll, wave-like, beneath you. This indicates a thin vegetation crust with water of unknown depth below. Do not break this crust, and gently retrace your steps to safe ground. If you go through then adopt the procedure detailed above as necessary.

Crossing Rivers and Streams

In most countries, but especially in Britain, hills mean rainfall and hence the presence of streams and rivers. Inevitably you will meet and wish to cross running water. From the smallest stream where the aim should be only to keep the feet dry, to the sizeable river where crossing can be a serious proposition, the correct technique must be used.

Firstly it must be made absolutely clear that a dry crossing is by far the most desirable. If a suitable bridge can be found then use it, even if this means making a considerable detour. If you use stepping stones or try boulder-hopping always consider what the result of a fall will be, and weigh any benefits against the risk of consequences of falling in. Even wet feet and boots can present serious problems in remote areas and sub-zero temperatures. If there is any chance of being swept downstream then forget this type of crossing.

Alternatively it may be possible to jump across the stream where it narrows, but again weigh up the likely consequences of not making it across. Remember, especially if wearing a rucksack, that you are not on the playing field in shorts and vest and judge your capability accordingly. You must also remember, if in a party, that it's a case of all across or none.

Remember too, when contemplating this type of jump crossing or using stepping stones, that in cold temperatures the river may be flowing freely with no signs of ice, but the rocks that have been splashed may be clad in clear, almost invisible, verglas. If this is the case your boot will slip off immediately with obvious (and potentially painful) consequences.

As a last resort you may consider that a wet crossing is the correct decision. If so you must carefully assess two things: the depth of the water and the strength of the current. A stick comes into its own here,

The power of water
Never underestimate this. Any depth of more than 1ft (300mm) can cause severe problems. A mountain stream does not have to be deep to be treacherous. Supercritical flow, a common occurrence in even quite shallow hill streams, is formidably powerful. When the river forms a pool or winds its way along the bottom of a valley it may appear sedate, but the saying 'still waters run deep' is often correct. Remember that mountain streams during periods of rain, distant storm in far hills or snow melt, rapidly become swollen torrents. That little stream you crossed a few hours ago can become uncrossable in these circumstances. Conversely they also fall quickly, and waiting for the right conditions can be preferable to forcing a crossing.

but if you cannot actually see the bottom then a wet crossing is to be avoided. Discolouration of the water or the rattling sound of stones being carried along indicate flood conditions and too strong a current – don't cross.

A mountain river or stream in spate is a much more serious proposition and all attempts should be made to seek a dry crossing (this photograph of the Sligachan Burn is taken from the bridge!) but if a wet crossing is decided on, the correct technique must be used.

Try the piggy-back
This technique always provides much amuse-ment. It is to be recomm-ended in non-serious situations on warm sunny days. The combined weight does add stability to the wader – so long as he does not lose his balance!

If you do decide to go ahead, follow this procedure:

- Pick an area where the stream bed is favourable; gravel or shingle should be chosen rather than slippery rocks
- Take your socks off but put your boots back on – this is essential to maintain balance
- Roll up clothing and reduce the drag as much as possible – clothing acts to the current as a sail to the wind, and this force alone can pull you into the water
- If waterproof overtrousers are left on then tie them at the ankle to keep them as streamlined as possible
- During a crossing a stick used as a third leg, both to feel the bottom and to assist balance, is extremely useful

The safest way for a group to cross is in a line, with arms linked, and with each member using a stick. Note that the line should be down the flow not across it. This is the most stable formation and means the person upstream will take the full force of the current but will provide a breakwater effect for those below. Those below are then in a stronger position to anchor themselves and support the upstream member. If all were strung out transversely across the stream then each would be subjected to the full strength of the current and the whole unit would be considerably weaker as a result.

A group crossing in line, aligned with the direction of the flow: here the group is firmly linked together both interlocking arms and grasping a pole in front. The important thing is that they are alighed with the direction fo flow which is the most stable configuration.

direction of flow

Crossing point selected for non-slippery, shingle/gravel bed (typically found at downstream end of pool).

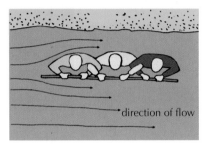

direction of flow

The upstream figure deflects the current, taking its full force and reducing the pressure on those downstream.The team have retained their boots but removed socks and trousers, so reducing drag. Arms are inerlinked and the pole held in fromt to form a strong unit.

If the worst happens and you are swept away:

- Relax; take air when possible but try to keep the water out of your mouth

- Remove the rucksack immediately. This is vital, and once off you will find that it floats and may provide an aid to buoyancy

- Go with the flow (as in scree running) – don't fight against it. Swim down with it but all the time aim to cross over to the nearest or most hospitable bank

- Avoid trees and branches that overhang (or are situated slightly below) the river's surface and could either knock you out or trap you as the current forces you underneath them

- Avoid jammed logs or other flood debris whenever possible.

Once a wet crossing has been made it is important not to get cold and possibly develop hypothermia (see Chapter 5, p. 122). Either change into dry clothes, and preferably have a hot drink, or keep moving.

***Solo crossing using a stick:** the walking stick or pole, or even a branch from the bank, is extremely useful here. It gives extra stability used as a third leg for balance and support. Additionally it is used to sound the depth and to probe the waters to determine the nature of the stream bed. Near Carnmore and Fionn Loch in the Fisherfield Forest, North West Highlands of Scotland.*

The hills in winter look particulary beautiful but be prepared for the many dangers. One must be aware of the potential dangers of winter hillwalking, have the correct equipment and be able to use it proficiently. Striding Edge, Helvellyn, the Lake District

Winter Walking

Those snow-clad peaks always look magnificent; indeed they are, and some of the most rewarding walks are to be had in these conditions. But never underestimate the dangers of venturing into the hills during the winter months; daylight hours are short, temperatures are low, the weather can turn ferociously with little warning, snow and ice conditions are complex and require the application of carefully practised techniques. It is imperative to your survival to be thoroughly prepared and equipped.

One of the most dangerous times – because it catches out the unwary – occurs when the hills do not have a particularly wintry appearance. The ground will be frozen solid and the steep slopes just as insecure as if they were covered in snow. Be on your guard, ready to apply all the following techniques, and go adequately equipped. Particularly recognise the significance of carrying, and being able to use, an ice axe – the importance of this cannot be overstated.

The correctly equipped winter walker: note the fact that even though the prevailing conditions do not merit the walker holding the axe here, it is readily available tucked over the shoulder between back and rucksack – it is immediately to hand without the walker having to stop to take off his rucksack. This is very imporant because many accidents result if the ice axe is not immediately available. Care must be taken when carrying the axe thus positioned, not to injure yourself or others with the exposed adze, pick or spike – particularly avoid poking the spike into your eye.

Clothing

Although this has already been discussed (Chapter 2), there are certain points that need to be carefully emphasised here. You need to be warm, weatherproof and windproof, but certain items of clothing (mere niceties in summer) are now absolutely essential for your safety and well-being. Gloves protect you from frostbite and frost nip. Remember to take with you a spare pair. If gloves are lost or irretrievably dropped, you subject yourself to the possibility of frostbite (which could cause the loss of your fingers) and also lose the ability to open your rucksack, tie laces and, most important of all, keep a firm grasp on your ice axe.

The woolly hat or equivalent is also very necessary. Much of your body heat is lost through the head, and ears must be protected from the icy wind. If things do not go according to plan and you are caught out as darkness falls the headtorch becomes a lifeline to survival. Check the battery each time before your walk; if it is at all low then replace it, and keep a spare bulb or bulbs in a safe but accessible place.

Starting Off

Carefully check that you have all the essential items of kit. Whilst you will most probably not require an ice axe or crampons when you start the walk they should be readily available for when the going begins to steepen. Place them where you can get them quickly and easily.

Different Conditions

The particular walking technique employed will depend on the conditions prevailing underfoot.

If the snow is soft and deep (if it is should you be on the hills? – see Chapter 1) walking can be exhausting. One member of the party should trailbreak, the most strenuous position, making the footsteps. The rest of the group should string along behind, using those footsteps and so conserving energy. If steps have been made previously, you are lucky and should use them. When the leader tires someone else should take his place.

Crusted snow can be the worst to walk on if the crust partially supports your weight and then breaks through as you lift the other foot. Beware of windslab avalanche when these conditions predominate. If a long trail is to be followed under these conditions then the value of skis or snow shoes should be assessed. (Britain seldom warrants the use of snow shoes, but there are many occasions when ski mountaineering is the best and easiest way to travel – but this is a complete subject in itself.) The only way crusted snow can be dealt with is by attempting to keep the crust intact, and it by no means always works. To do this distribute and lessen the load as you place your feet and transfer your load onto them.

When the ground steepens, it is time to have your axe in, or immediately ready to, hand and crampons on the boots.

Using the Ice Axe for Assistance

Remember ice axes are sharp; the spike, pick and adze are all capable of inflicting injury on you or others if they are used improperly. Whether you use the wrist strap or not is your decision – there are numerous arguments for and against. For example, you don't wish to lose it if it drops from your hand, but conversely if you slip and let go of it, it can be very dangerous left attached. Consider your particular circumstances carefully.

The ice axe:
This is essential for all winter walks, and can be used to assist and steady progress when climbing, descending or traversing snow. Equally effectively it can be used to cross a single patch of ice or penetrate hard frozen ground. Its chief function is to arrest a fall, and many times it is the axe alone that has the ability to save you.

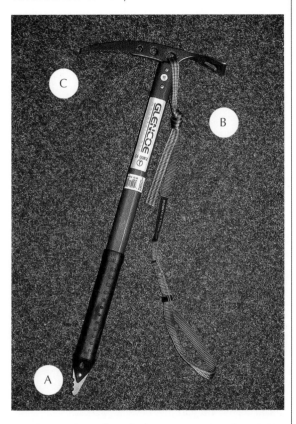

*The ice axe and its component parts: each part of the ice axe has its own particular function. **A** The SPIKE is used as a walking stick, and **B** the ADZE for cutting steps and the **C** the PICK for sticking into snow and ice, either as a means of progress or during ice axe arrest.*

The axe can be used as a means of assisting progress in a number of ways. Using the spike is the most common way during a non-technical hillwalking outing. The axe is held and used as a walking stick, with the spike and shaft implanted into the snow for security. During ascent it is often pushed in and then the weight is placed with the hand holding the head rather than gripping the shaft. This applies equally to descent; remember to bend the legs as much as possible when descending.

The pick is generally only used for steep ground (45 degrees upwards) or for ice-axe breaking (see below). But situations can occur on a winter hill walk, albeit infrequently, where the pick is used:

- Swing the axe like a hammer (the pick is in effect the hammer head) to lodge the pick in the snow (which must be sufficiently hard) or ice. The shaft is then used as a handhold

- Alternatively the head of the axe is used as a handhold. When one hand grips the shaft and the other the head this technique is known as piolet ancre, and is useful for traversing around an awkward corner

- Another technique employing the pick in descent is to swing the axe and place the pick below you. You then use the shaft as a handrail – it is useful for moving over short sections of hard steep ice or snow, and should really be combined with the use of crampons to prevent the feet slipping

Unless the snow is particularly firm, in which case the adze can be used in a similar manner to the pick as described above, the adze is chiefly used to cut steps in the snow or ice. This is only necessary if you are not wearing crampons. The type of step depends on your circumstances, but fashion them so they are safe to use, that is, they are sufficiently large and slope into the hill so your foot slides to a safe edge and not out of the hold. Cutting a series of steps is tiring work and is an art in itself – you may only need the odd step for extra security.

Self Arrest – Ice-Axe Braking

This is the main reason for carrying an ice axe and it is the only way you will be able to stop if you slip on a steep snow slope. It is a relatively easy technique but it must be practised until you are competent and can do it with total confidence. It consists of a number of stages which are best explained pictorially.

Ice axe techniques – using the spike: the four different uses of the axe shown here constitute those most useful in hillwalking.

The most common use of the ice axe is as shown with the spike prodded into the snow. The axe you choose should be suitably long to enable you to to this without stooping.

During an ascent on snow, prod in the spike and shaft and push down on the head. Kick the boots in to make steps. Note how the pick faces into the slope ready to adopt the ice-braking position in the event of a fall.

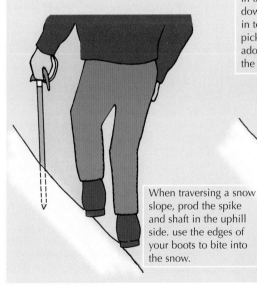

When traversing a snow slope, prod the spike and shaft in the uphill side. use the edges of your boots to bite into the snow.

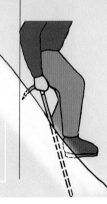

During a descent on snow, prod in the spike and shaft and hold the head. Note how the pick faces into the slope. Stamp in the boot heels to make steps.

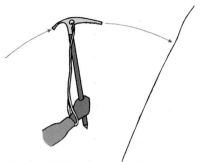

*Ice axe techniques –
using the pick: it is
only usual to use the
pick, as shown here,
when the going
begins to get steep.
the essential thing is
to give the axe a
good swing to firmly
embed the pick. It
requires practice
and experience to
develop the*

Placing the pick into the snow is done swinging the ice axe and holding the base of the shaft. Give a good, firm, confident swing, planting the pick well into the snow (or ice). This is when a well-balanced ice axe will be really appreciated.

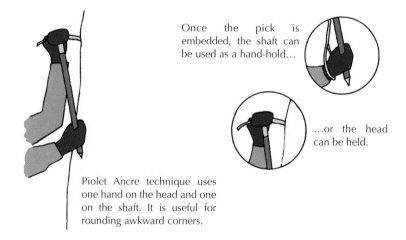

Once the pick is embedded, the shaft can be used as a hand-hold...

...or the head can be held.

Piolet Ancre technique uses one hand on the head and one on the shaft. It is useful for rounding awkward corners.

In descent, when the axe has been placed with pick inserted as shown, the shaft can be used as a handrail. this is useful for negotiating short patches of ice or hard show when crampons are worn. Note how the knees are bent and the walker stoops low to grip the shaft. Once below the head of the shaft, the axe is removed and inserted lower down the slope.

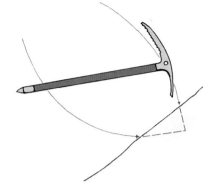

Ice axe techniques – using the adze: *primarily the adze is used to cut steps if crampons are not worn. Both the edges and the end of the axe can be used and you should attempt to economise your effort. Make the step large enough and with the base sloping towards the hill so that your good will not slip out.*

Axe correctly held in the braking position: *when you fall, resist the temptation to let go of our axe. Hold it across the chest thus, one hand on the head and one hand on the shaft. This position can be gained after one has slipped but it is always better to anticipate a slip and have the pick pointing in the direction of the slope.*

The slip has occurred and the ice axe is held ready: *sliding down the slope the ice axe is positioned correctly across the chest. The next stage is to roll over onto your front.*

If you should fall

You may start to roll or somersault. Relax if you can, but control this by gradually opening out your body until you are stretched out horizontal on the slope. Now is the time to start the ice-axe braking procedure. It doesn't matter if you are not in the position shown (head up) for if you are head down (facing in or out); adopt the technique given here and you will swing round to the correct braking position automatically.

The full braking position: the pick is pressed into the snow. Keep the adze away from your face, a common mistake with beginners is to forget this and cut the face with its sharp edge. (Although experienced users may situate the axe more under the body applying body weight to adjust the pressure on the pick, you must first practise the fall in the position shown which will not result in a cut face from the adze. it is possible to vary the speed of descent by varying the weight on the pick. Note how the back is arched and the feet are up in the air – is is absolutely essential if wearing crampons otherwise the crampon points stick, while you do not, and consequently you either snap your ankle or you are thrown into the air. Wearing boots without crampons makes this consideration less critical.

Sliding head-first down the slope
Stage 1: the pick of the axe is dug in out to to one side.

Stage 2: the body automatically pivots round

Stage 3: without any further action the correct braking position is attained. The procedure is exactly the same when upside down (see over).

Sliding upside down head-first down the slope

Stage 1: place the ice axe pick out to the side as shown here and you automatically turn into the correct braking position just as above. It feels weird at first but it does work very effectively and could save you from serious injury – practise it.

Stage 2: the body automatically pivots round.

Stage 3: the correct braking position

Crampon Work

Crampons are useful (if not essential) for winter walking if the snow is hard, if there is ice or if the ground is frozen. Firstly ensure that crampons and boots are suitably matched. Secondly the fastening of boots to crampons must be adequate and secure. Make sure that these two criteria are fully met before you leave the shop with your crampons.

_Crampon work whilst traversing or ascending__: the technique is to flex the ankle so that all the base points of the crampons bite into the slope._

The basic technique for the walker, as opposed to the climber tackling steep ground, is to keep all the base points in contact with the slope. This requires flexing of the ankle on anything other than horizontal ground, to place the crampon parallel to the slope. When traversing and ascending it is important _not_ to use the edge of the boot (as you would if you were using boots without crampons) but to keep _all_ the base points of the crampons in contact with the slope. Likewise when descending keep all the base points in contact. _Do not_ dig in the heels (as you would if wearing boots without crampons). Crampons must be placed firmly, not half-heartedly; stamp them into the snow or ice with some

Crampon work whilst traversing or descending: *again, all the base points should be stamped into the slope by flexing the ankles. Notice particularly how the fronts of the crampons point directly down the slope. Whilst using crampons in descent, resist the temptation to dig in the heels only.*

Using the crampon front points in steep ascent: *here only the two points that stick out at the front are kicked into the slope. It enables a rapid ascent to be made and feels more natural than other forms of crampon work. It does, however, place a great strain on boots and calf muscles.*

assertion. This and the technique of flexing the ankle requires much practice to perfect.

During steep ascent, and if your crampons have them (not all walking crampons do), you can kick in the two front points of each crampon and use these for support (along with a suitable ice-axe technique as shown above). This is known as 'front pointing' and is a climbing technique that enables rapid ascent to be made without the necessity of cutting steps or flexing the ankles.

But it must be stressed that the most important single item of equipment for the winter hillwalker is the ice axe. Own one, carry it where it is immediately accessible, and master the technique of using it. Crampons do have their uses, for example on a mountain slope turned to hard ice – blasted by a freezing wind – or crossing frozen ground, but there are a number of problems that should be appreciated by the aspiring crampon user:

- Care must be taken not to spike one's own legs or those of others.

- Boots and crampons must be compatible and firmly securable.

- They must be sufficiently rugged to be worn over mixed ground (over rock as well as snow).

- They have a tendency to 'ball up' in soft snow – that is, to build up a layer of snow on the bottom which eventually acts like a toboggan unless you systematically knock them with the ice axe to dislodge the snow. This is a common cause of accidents.

- When ice-axe braking it is imperative to remember to arch the back and lift the feet, so crampons do not stick. A crampon spiking the slope in these circumstance can, and often does, lead to serious injury.

Enjoy your winter walking, but practise the techniques well.

Near the crest of Aonach Eagach Ridge, Glencoe, West Highlands of Scotland

The hills give us tremendous freedom – many only feel truly at home in these steep, wild places. But along with an appreciation of their great beauty there must be an awareness of the limitless force of nature. Remember that the mountains give and the mountains take.

Whilst the best possible means of staying safe on the hills is by utilising the techniques already detailed and avoiding potentially dangerous situations, unfortunate incidents can and do occur. If you are prepared and are aware of potential danger, if you know how to deal with hazards as they arise and, if necessary, can utilise the help of others, you will enjoy a long and happy life in the hills. Underestimate their awesome potential and your enjoyment will be cut short.

I regard correct survival technique in the hills as a circular procedure starting in the safety of the civilised world and only ending when you return. All stages are progressive and interrelated, and it is necessary to appreciate the concept as a whole. Before we go there should be a period of anticipation, where we plan and prepare ourselves accordingly. Adaption is the period when, faced by dangerous circumstances and natural hazards, we recognise the problems and utilise the correct techniques to survive. If an accident occurs we may need to summon the help of others – this can be recognised as a time of association. So this formula for survival (AAA) consists of three recognisable functions:

- **Anticipation**
- **Adaption**
- **Association**

ANTICIPATION: BEING PREPARED

Along with all that has been said already regarding correct equipment, assessment of difficulty and adoption of suitable technique, it is important to stress that your well-being and survival depends primarily on you. Tackling the hills and steep remote places requires a degree of both physical fitness and mental toughness.

Physical Fitness and Mental Toughness

Do not attempt a long and difficult walk with no escape potential unless you are physically fit to do so. The best training for walking is to walk. If you live in

In winter the combined effects of cold, adverse weather, soft snow and early darkness can make a day on the a grim battle for survival: Jack's Rake on Pavey Ark above Great Langdale, the Lake District.

the city walk in the evening or during the lunch hour.

Mental toughness requires you firstly to accept responsibility and then endure any hardships which your goal requires within safety limits. You must be prepared to adapt rapidly to changing circumstances and maintain a realistic and logical assessment. However good your equipment, the mainstay of your self-preservation is sound judgement. Never give in, whatever the circumstances – if you tell yourself that you are going to survive you will.

Food and Drink

You burn energy quickly in the hills, and the body requires fuel no matter what its performance. Always prepare adequate and suitable food and drink for your walk. Carry the food that you expect to eat during the day (see below) and additionally a reserve of relatively light high-energy food for use in an emergency or survival situation.

The rules are:

- Take enough food and drink to replace lost energy during the day

- Have reserve capacity of high-energy food to sustain you if caught out

Chocolate bars and boiled sugar-type sweets are light and compact and help replace vital energy. If you are undertaking a day's walk something more substantial should be taken, and sandwiches are a favourite meal on the hills. They should be made to provide good food/weight value. Bear in mind that for a day's walk of reasonable length in the hills you will burn up something in the order of 5000 calories. It is important too to start with a good breakfast inside you – for the hillwalker this is the most important meal of the day. It provides a high blood sugar level which will sustain you, with the correct topping up, throughout the day.

The amount of drink you need to carry depends on the prevailing weather conditions and on the availability of clean drinking water on the hill. Do not underestimate the body's fluid requirements in hot dry conditions, but with a little planning and careful observation most of this will be found during the course of the day. There is nothing quite like drinking from a cool fresh mountain spring on a hot day, but watch out for pollution – never drink downstream of man or his works and watch out for dead animals and so on fouling the water source. Carrying a warm drink is well worth the little extra weight that a thermos flask entails – in cold conditions its warming properties can work wonders. A pinch of salt (or a salt tablet) taken separately from the drink eases and prevents the effects of cramp.

The reserve capacity food should be kept separately, in the flap of your rucksack for example, and not consumed until it is certain you are going to arrive at your intended destination. If caught out on the hills this food may keep you alive. There was once an accident in the Lake District where a solo walker

Leave a note

When you go off into the hills you must have a definite plan and you must tell others just what this is. Inform people in your accommodation base just what you intend to do and your intended time of return. Always leave a note in the car windscreen (so it can be clearly read from the outside) stating your name(s), the date and time of leaving and concise, unambiguous details of your intended route and the estimated time of your return. If you meet unexpected difficulties, or an accident occurs resulting in your failure to return in a reasonable time, this information will prove invaluable.

fell down a gully, broke his leg and could not get out. He was missing for some 30 days after which he was found alive, sustained for all this time by a single packet of biscuits in his rucksack. He made a full recovery!

Dealing with Natural Hazards

Once out in the hills there are many hazards that can be experienced and deserve particular attention. An awareness of these and the correct techniques to be adopted should they be encountered will ensure your survival.

Falling Rocks

Always be on the lookout for falling rocks on the hills; they are not uncommon. Rain loosens and softens them, and they can cut loose without further assistance. The warm sun thawing frozen ground or snow and ice also releases rockfall. Hill animals dislodge rocks, and in Britain sheep are particularly merciless. People can be careless; always be wary of

Looking out over the rocky high tops of the Lake District. A landscape full of hazards. The nearby ravine of Piers Gill once entrapped a lone walker for thirty days before he was rescued alive, having survived on a solitary packet of biscuits. Over Pikes Crag to Lingmell with shapely Great Gable seen beyond

others above you. If you accidentally dislodge a stone (even of quite moderate size) then always loudly shout, 'Below'.

The first warning of a falling rock or rocks will nearly always be the crashing noise as they pound down – there is often little time to react, so you must move quickly even if you cannot actually see the danger. If on steep ground get as near as you can into the slope of rock in front of you. Protect your head by placing your forearms over the top and spreading your fingers over the back, or get your rucksack off and place this over it if there is enough time. If you know you have time seek rock or tree shelter.

Lightning

Lightning storms are not exceptional in the hills and deaths do occur. Statistics show that there is little cause for concern, but there are definite do's and don'ts. Probably there will not be a great deal of time to move far when a lightning storm threatens but an effort should be made to get into an open space away from those features that will attract lightning strike.

Observing the lightning flash and then counting the delay between this and the subsequent roll of thunder will give an indication of how far away the storm is and, by taking a series of these counts, in which direction it is travelling; sound travels at a rate of approximately 1km per 3sec. This may enable you to follow the safest course of action as detailed below.

The walker is particularly vulnerable whilst on the sharp edges of ridges, gullies or ravines, especially those that run down from prominent features such as a ridge or pinnacle. Standing beneath obvious conductors should be avoided; under a tree is probably the most dangerous position of all but the same principle applies to rock pinnacles. Sheltering in a small cave or under boulders is bad practice, as is taking cover in a rock crevice or fissure in the ground, because when lightning strikes it runs along the ground and jumps these gaps.

So during a lightning storm you should:

- Forget about seeking natural shelter from the rain
- Find a relatively open space and sit down or kneel low on your rucksack
- Attempt to keep the minimum contact with the ground and do not put your hands down on the ground for support
- Walking sticks or ice axes are best placed on the

If you are unlucky
Sometimes, particularly if near a ridge or on an exposed section of summit, you may experience a tingling sensation, even to the extent that your hair will become charged and literally stand on end! Don't panic, and follow the advice given here as best you can. If you should be so unlucky as to actually be struck by lightning then there is still little likelihood that it will prove fatal. As a final word of comfort there are some who can boast(!) that they have been struck by lightning three times – and survived.

ground by the side or some distance away from you, but don't discard them altogether – you will need them when the storm dissipates

It may be cold comfort to know, as hillwalkers, that probably the safest place to be during a lightning storm is in your car.

Do sit on a rucksack in relatively open space. Lay ice axe or walking stick to one side. Keep hands and feet off the ground.

Don't stand in an exposed position. Get down from ridges and paths.

Don't stand in gullies or ravines.

Don't shelter in caves

Don't crawl beneath boulders.

Don't hide in holes or rock fissures.

Don't shelter beneath a tree.

Don't stand by a rock pinnacle.

Don't hold a stick or ice axe in the air.

Snake and Insect Bites

The seriousness of bites depends on where you are. Exotic, far-flung localities require careful research and preparation. In Britain and much of Western Europe the danger from snake bite is minimal. The adder is the chief culprit, but you have to be very unlucky (some would say lucky) firstly to find a snake and secondly to attract its attention. If left alone there is really no danger for they are afraid of man. The chief danger lies in catching them unawares or standing on them. However, they are very sensitive to vibration; if you are walking through deep bracken or heather a wise and effective precaution is to stamp the feet or slap the rock (or a tree trunk) periodically as you move along. If you are about to take a rest always double-check before you sit on that clump of heather. Likewise, if stooping through branches keep a wary eye open.

In Britain only the adder is venomous; although grass snakes do strike and bite, they are not poisonous. Seldom, however, does the actual snake encountered look anything like the one shown in the textbook. The best advice is simply to leave all snakes alone.

Again in Britain there are few biting insects that can cause real health problems. However, they can make life a misery, particularly the infamous Scottish midge (at its very worst on the Isle of Skye in August!). It very much depends on your sensitivity – some people are affected much worse than others – but in any case a suitable midge and mosquito repellent is recommended. Planning your trips according to season is also a sound precaution.

Coping with snake bite
In the unlikely event that you are bitten by an adder, the effects are usually slight, and if you are fit and healthy you will not come to any lasting harm. The procedure when bitten is to stay calm, do not start to run or get excited, and make your way directly back to medical help. The effects will most probably be that the affected limb will become painful and swollen and there may be symptoms of shock.

Wild Plants and Poisoned Water Sources

Although there are quite a few edible plants on the hills, unless you know exactly what you are doing (from first-hand experience and not just from book information), it is wisest to leave them well alone. Some plants are absolutely deadly and many of these are quite common (deadly nightshade in Britain, for example) – often the most attractive plants are the worst offenders.

If you drink be absolutely certain that the water is unpolluted and only ever drink from running water of wholesome appearance. In some areas the rocks contain naturally poisonous mineral salts. A recent major concern, which cannot be seen, and the full effects of which nobody yet knows, is radioactive contamination. The wise precaution must be, 'If in doubt, don't drink'.

Effects of the Sun

Quite apart from the amount of liquid you will lose in sunny conditions, which must always be replaced to avoid heat exhaustion, the sun brings other problems. Sunburn should never be underestimated and it is always wise to protect the sensitive areas with cream, not forgetting the backs of the legs. Travel on snow or glaciers heightens the effects of the sun and stronger cream (glacier cream) is necessary. Areas to watch are the nose, the tips of the ears and the lips.

Also be wary of the powerful effects of ultra-violet rays reflected from the snow – always wear glacier goggles or suitably protective sunglasses to avoid snow-blindness. Although this is a temporary condition it strikes with little warning, and this is its main danger. After a short exposure all that will be felt is an irritation or itching in the eye. This is followed rapidly by the painful feeling that sand is being rubbed continuously in your eyes, and you cannot open them. Obviously to be blinded on the hills is very serious. Seek medical advice, but rest in a darkened environment is a necessary part of any cure.

Thin Ice

It is always possible, if walking on snow disguising ice, to break through thin ice. The shock of hitting water just above freezing point is considerable (for the effects and treatment of hypothermia see below) and it is important to keep fighting. If possible retain hold of the ice and remove your rucksack which may give some aid to buoyancy. Try to ease your weight onto the unbroken ice, spreading it over as wide an area as possible. If it breaks again keep up the procedure in the direction of the bank (if this is known). The ice may become thicker and more supportive, or the water may become sufficiently shallow for you to walk along the bottom.

To assist someone who has broken through the ice takes courage, but it can be done by spreading your load. Lie on the ice, preferably with a jacket (or if available long flat planks of wood) beneath you and it reduces the point (breaking through) loading on the ice. If you bear in mind that until the victim went through the ice it supported his weight, and you spread your load over a wider area, then it is possible to reach and assist the victim. The actual helping should be done either with an outstretched stick or at arm's length.

Crossing ice can be extremely hazardous. Have a mental strategy prepared should the ice break. Three Tarns, Bowfell, the Lake District

Falling through thin ice

If you are unlucky enough to break through thin ice and sink in the water you will float back up again; try to aim for the hole you have made. If you don't reach it but are washed away then be aware that there is always an air gap between the surface of the water and the ice, and aim to get your nose in this air space. Where the water moves there are generally 'blow holes' in the ice and these should be sought.

Avalanche

These occur much more frequently than is popularly believed. Massive movements of snow can occur even on slopes of moderate steepness. It is a complex subject, but often even the experts are caught out – avalanches often flaunt all the rules with devastating consequences. The most important step is to avoid venturing forth in potential avalanche conditions. Some of these have been highlighted already, but be wary of the hills when:

- There is fresh snow (at least 24 hours should be allowed after snowfall before one ventures onto the hills, and a period of three days or more is preferable)

- There is an accumulation of blown or soft snow above you (be particularly careful under cliffs and when entering narrow valleys or gullies)

- Conditions are right for a thaw, when large masses of snow and ice can be released from the heights and can travel remarkable distances

- A thin hard snow crust only covers softer powder snow or hailstones (which act like ballbearings) below

To detect avalanche potential when on the hills is difficult – if conditions feel at all dodgy (and sometimes you just get the feeling when shivers run down the back of the neck) *get off the hill*. Always seek local advice on both conditions and locality. Many locations in the hills are specifically known to avalanche regularly. It is also possible to dig an avalanche detection pit with your axe. Simply dig a trench with a vertical side wall then go down this wall testing the hardness of the snow every few inches by prodding with your fingers. If you find a weak plane, softer snow underlying harder snow above, or soft snow above unbound to a hard surface below, then stay away. Alternatively, without digging a pit, the snow can be prod-tested from above using the shaft of the axe. Try to get the whole of the shaft in, probing as deep as possible, and if softer layers are found then the same advice applies – get off the hill.

ACCIDENT AND RESCUE

If the worst happens and an accident occurs the situation must first be correctly identified and then, if necessary, the help of others called upon. There are a number of basic techniques that must be learnt to effectively

Caught in an avalanche
If this happens there is only a limited amount you can do. Try to swim along with the flow and make the greatest effort to reach the surface and create an air space, as you feel the movement stop and tighten. Really fight here, for these last few seconds of action can be vital. If any of your party is buried it is correct procedure to probe with axe or ski pole to attempt to locate them. This should be done in a logical systematic manner so you know precisely the ground covered. If, in a reasonable time, you cannot locate them, mark their most likely position (so it can be seen from a helicopter if necessary) and seek assistance.

achieve this. This section will cover these and ranges from first aid to summoning and coordinating rescue.

Never give in, no matter how bad your particular circumstances appear – adopt this philosophy and you will survive. However, never underestimate the seriousness of your situation or the dangers of shock or exhaustion. Reassure the victim: be sympathetic and caring, but firm if necessary.

Crossing Broad Crag, The Scafell Massif, the Lake District

Hypothermia

When a person gets tired and loses body heat and energy he is susceptible to the next stage of deterioration which is now referred to as hypothermia (once known as exposure). This is an extremely dangerous condition and needs to be rapidly diagnosed. It will probably start with the victim shivering and lagging behind. As the condition becomes more acute the victim loses the ability to be logical and accurately assess the situation. This should be recognised by other members of the group. Stop and rest the victim, keeping him as warm and insulated from the elements as possible. In most cases a warm, sugary drink and energy foods are helpful. If necessary go and get help.

First Aid

A victim should be kept as warm as possible and should be protected from the elements. It may be necessary to construct a temporary shelter or windbreak. Render first aid, but if the injured person shows any sign of suffering spinal damage *do not move*. Spinal damage may be expected if the victim is suffering from a pain in the back or an inability to move the legs.

All hill users should attend a basic first aid course, and the following notes are a very basic guide only. It is desirable to always have in your rucksack a simple first-aid kit consisting of at least plasters, lint and antiseptic cream. When an accident occurs be systematic and check breathing and airways and look for bleeding and broken bones.

- If breathing has stopped clear the throat and pull the tongue forwards. Give mouth-to-mouth resuscitation if needed: open the mouth by pressing on the chin. Pinch the nose and blow into the mouth. Effort is needed and you must check to ensure the chest is rising as you blow. If there is no pulse combine mouth-to-mouth resuscitation with cardiac massage which is quite simple but requires qualified tuition.

- Bleeding can be stopped by applying pressure to the wound through a suitable pad, which could be an item of clothing or a handkerchief. Press this firmly onto the wound for about 10 minutes.

- Swelling or deformity and localised pain indicate broken bones. Immobilise the limb for this prevents both further damage and reduces pain.

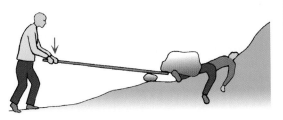

Leg trapped beneath a boulder

The lever principle: if 'l' is twice the distance of 'Y' then the lifting force you exert on a fallen rock is twice that of the load you push down with. Hence it is possible to life extremely heavy objects with ease.

Lifting heavy objects
Using the principle of levers to lift heavy objects if, for example, someone is trapped, has been referred to in Chapter 4. But it has numerous practical applications. Quite simply it involves using a sufficiently stout long pole or tree branch as a lever – the longer the lever the greater the load that can be lifted – and is done as illustrated here.

Rescue Procedure – Getting Help

Distress signalling

If you cannot move from the accident location you may have to summon help by use of an internationally recognisable distress signal. This can be done by torch or whistle or by shouting to anyone who is nearby.

International SOS: Torch light or whistle – give three short flashes (blasts on the whistle), three long flashes, and then three short flashes. Repeat after a one-minute interval.

This signal should be acknowledged by three flashes in rapid succession which are repeated at minute intervals.

When a decision has been made that self-help alone is not enough to rectify the situation, rescue must be summoned. The recent advent of mobile phone technology, particularly in the case of solo hill walkers, has proved invaluable. To contact the rescue services (in Britain) simply dial 999 and ask for the police. Keep calm and give the required information clearly and accurately. Your location on the hill is absolutely vital to minimise the rescue effort. Giving a map coordinate is obviously ideal, as is a concise and accurate description. Think of the important locators, working down from the most obvious, such as, 'I'm on Scafell Pike and have fallen descending to the col below Broad Crag. I was heading north east back to Esk Hause and Langdale'. If you are confused take a little time and try to tell your tale from the beginning. The police in turn will contact the mountain rescue. Of course, with this power of communication comes a great deal of responsibility. If you phone the police they have to call out the rescue services no matter what – so do not make that decision lightly.

For those without a mobile phone, if more than one in the party are in good shape, a fit member should be left to look after the injured party whilst others seek help. If the victim must be left alone ensure the position is adequately marked. Leave something bright and large on the ground so that it can be seen from both ground and the air. If possible the victim should occupy a site, clearly marked, which is suitably clear and open for air rescue by helicopter. Any loose equipment/clothing should be weighted down or secured to prevent it being swept away by the helicopter's downdraft (or alternatively sucked up into its engine vents).

Before you leave the scene of the accident note the location and its features and make sure you know the position on the map precisely. Get other members of the party to check and confirm this, and you should all note the grid reference and time of departure. All these facts are vital to the rescue services when you contact them. If possible, two fit members of the party should be sent to summon help. To contact the rescue services phone the emergency services (dial 999 at any telephone – ask for the police –-no money is needed).

Carrying Victims

If it is desirable to carry the victim out without seeking assistance, the technique depends on the number of available hands in the party. If there are two of you – yourself and the victim – it may be possible to adopt a piggy-back technique. You will have to be fit and strong or there will be two victims! By lengthening the shoulder straps on your rucksack it should be possible for the victim to squeeze in between the rucksack and your back with legs over the bottom of the straps – this saves considerable energy (avoiding the necessity to hold on, which rapidly becomes tiring).

If there are at least two members of the party who are fit and well then it may be best to form a stretcher. One of the simplest can be made from two poles of suitable length and two anoraks. Simply thread the poles through the body of the first garment and out of the sleeves, then thread on the next garment with the sleeves nearest the other end of the poles – and you have an efficient and practical stretcher.

Forced Bivouacs

If it is absolutely necessary to spend the night on the hill then the main requirements are to insulate yourself from the ground and form a windbreak. (If a bivouac is planned a karrimat or equivalent to insulate and a sleeping bag to retain warmth are essential). It should only be necessary to bivouac if you are absolutely exhausted. In summer you can take shelter, under a boulder for example, and use your rucksack to insulate you from the ground.

In winter it is vital to get out of the wind. If forced to spend time out in the snow – say a blizzard hits and you can move no further – then scoop out a dish in the snow and use your rucksack to block off the wind as best you can. It is even better to dig out a snow cave with your ice axe and this is an effective way to shelter from the cold and wind.

Digging a snow cave: *the correct procedure is as shown here*

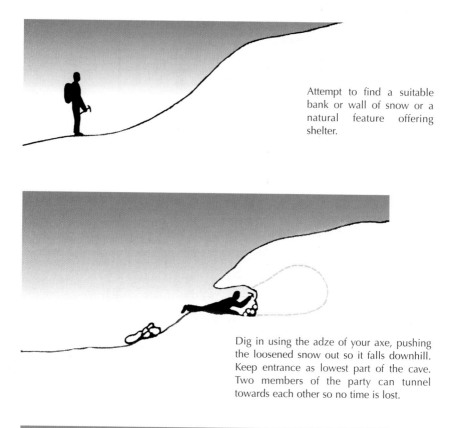

Attempt to find a suitable bank or wall of snow or a natural feature offering shelter.

Dig in using the adze of your axe, pushing the loosened snow out so it falls downhill. Keep entrance as lowest part of the cave. Two members of the party can tunnel towards each other so no time is lost.

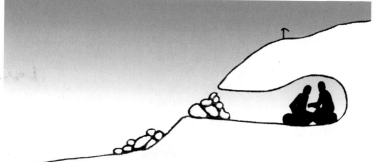

Sit or lie on rucksacks for insulation. Huddle together to preserve warmth. Mark the top of the cave with the axe so you can be located. Block entrance with snow as necessary.

Crossing Broad Slack on the Greenburn Horseshoe, Southern Fells, the Lake District

The view west to Beinn Alligan from Mighty Liathach,
Torridon Hills, North West Scotland

PHOTOGRAPHY

For me, photography is one of the great joys of being out in the wild open spaces. To stand on some high hillside early on a spring morning with the world below hidden beneath a sea of cloud, and the high peaks glowing gold in the rays of the rising sun, is a wonderful experience. Capturing moments such as these, whether to create an artistic or imaginative image or merely to record a memorable movement for posterity, is a naturally complementary and thrilling opportunity.

At its best landscape photography is an art form that demands not only accomplished technique but flair and imagination. The essential techniques and applications of modern hill photography must be studied and practised until they become second nature, but the ability to capture an image that transcends the mere record photograph depends on the eye and the heart of the individual photographer.

The scope of mountain photography is vast, and amongst its subjects should be included not only the obvious landscape work but also the human element, ranging from the positioning and movement of groups to expressive portraits. In addition to this many hillwalking photographers specialise in certain natural subjects – perhaps butterflies, or geology, or a particular type of lighting situation. Whatever your own particular interest the pursuit of photography in the hills is tremendous fun.

I have my own favourite subjects, for example capturing the wonderful evening light when the valleys are black, the peaks red, and the sky ranges through almost every colour between. It is often possible to recognise the work of an individual photographer by their particular style. When a photographer who has reached this stage of performance takes a photograph, there is no conscious thought about the many technicalities required to achieve a good image. Camera and eye are one, and the actual mechanics of the photography become second nature.

However, to reach this elevated state of the art requires both a sound understanding of all the principles involved, including a thorough knowledge of all the different items of equipment that can be used to create a good photograph, and the practical ability to apply that knowledge. Remember that one must crawl before one can walk and the accomplished photographer must put in time and hard work to become proficient in the art.

BASICS

There are some basic principles that are so simple, it is surprising how many 'would-be' photographers fail to appreciate their value. They are fundamental and deserve careful consideration.

Firstly, a hillwalker should always have immediate and convenient access to his equipment. Correct carrying of all equipment, lenses, filters and cameras is vitally important and will be dealt with later – cameras buried deep in sacs will not be used and that unique opportunity will be lost.

Secondly, all images must be correctly exposed and sharp. If not, they are not photographs, but mistakes.

Thirdly, the hillwalker must be able to carry all his equipment throughout the walk. It is no good having all the latest superb and expensive high-tech gear if it is not light, practicable to use on the hills and durable. Extra items of gear can sound terrific in the magazines, but the simplest and lightest equipment will provide the hillwalker with the maximum amount of pleasure.

Fourthly, it should be appreciated that light is everything in photography. The difference between a flat landscape and an exciting visual adventure can simply be the prevailing light conditions. The ability to be at the right place at the right time to capture the optimum lighting effect is one of the most important aspects of mountain photography.

THE CAMERA

What It Does

Bear in mind that in this world of high-tech gadgetry the most perfect image that can be reproduced is that made by a simple pinhole camera – no lenses, no shutter, no electronics – just the application of the natural laws of physics. A camera records an image on film and, despite any degree of sophistication, there are only two considerations that affect the image quality in any given situation. These are correct focus and correct exposure of the image onto the film. There's nothing else; so do not be misled by powerful sales hype.

- Correct focus can be achieved by adjusting the lens in and out

- Correct exposure is obtained by controlling the quantity of light reaching the film, which is achieved by two variables; the action of matching the shutter speed (the period during which the light stays on the film, ranging typically from 1 second to 1/2000 of a second) with the aperture (measured typically from f22 (narrowest opening) to f2.8 (widest opening, letting in most light through the lens)

Types of Camera

There are a number of different format cameras available, but for the mobile hillwalker requiring a lightweight camera with a choice of lenses and ancillary equipment 35mm is the most suitable and popular format. This figure refers to the size of the image made by the camera on the film; the actual image is rectangular, and measures 35mmx24mm.

Brocken Spectre seen from Scar Crags, North Western Fells, the Lake District

Lightweight Miniatures

There are many lightweight miniature cameras of 35mm format on the market and these are extremely useful for the walker and mountaineer. The correct choice of this type of camera can give the hillwalker a very powerful tool capable of producing excellent results. However, most are described as 'fully electronic and automatic', which in practical terms means that they are of fixed focus, relying on the depth of field of a wide angle lens to achieve focus, and on electronic metering and control of aperture to give correct exposure. Whilst I in no way dismiss this type of camera they do have serious limitations.

Depending on what you pay, the lens quality can be superb and the technological sophistication immense. But, perhaps surprisingly, it is this latter quality that can be disadvantageous. Most of these fully electronic and automatic cameras expose the photograph by using a system known as *centre weighted metering* which means they take the average amount of light from a scene and correctly expose for this. Because of the difficult nature of hillwalking photography, with bright sky and dark landscape, it most often means that the average exposure taken by these cameras is unsuitable for the composition – the sky will be overexposed (washed out) and the hills underexposed (too dark). Therefore it is desirable to obtain a lightweight miniature 35mm camera on which, despite the centre weighted metering, you can set the exposure (shutter speed and aperture setting) yourself.

It is still possible to obtain a miniature camera with built-in exposure meter, which does not depend on electronics, that is a fully mechanical camera that does not require batteries, and this is the type of miniature camera most suited for serious hillwalking and mountain photography. If one cannot find a fully mechanical camera then my second choice would be one where, despite the fact that metering is done electronically, the shutter speed and the aperture setting can be chosen by the photographer.

Reflex Cameras

A reflex camera allows the photographer to see through the eyepiece the exact image that will be exposed onto the film. This is achieved by taking the light that passes through the lens to the eyepiece by reflecting it up through a mirror – when the shutter is pressed and the photo is taken the mirror flips out of the way and the exact image seen by the photographer hits the film.

The 35mm *single lens reflex (SLR) camera* with built-in light metering system is the wisest choice for most hillwalking situations. Correctly selected they are both lightweight and durable, offering a wide variety of interchangeable lenses and other ancillary equipment. Advances in electronic technology have led to a remarkable degree of sophistication and the choices available can confuse even the expert. The best advice I can offer is simply to understand the basic fundamental requirements of hillwalking photography and not be overawed by the modern technology – just select what is beneficial to you.

The following considerations are the most important in choosing and using the camera for hillwalking photography – all the rest you can make up your own mind about!

Electronic or Mechanical

It is becoming increasingly difficult to obtain all-mechanical cameras, and quite often those that are mechanical still depend on batteries to operate their metering systems. Nevertheless, despite working in sub-zero conditions with all-electronic cameras, I have never experienced problems with battery failure but have, on a number of occasions, found the battery drained due to the system being inadvertently switched on whilst being carried. Keep the camera beneath your jacket, near to body heat when not in use. Carry a spare set of batteries, but remember that they only have limited life even when not in use. Some electronic cameras will operate mechanically on a single selected shutter speed even when the batteries fail and this can be a worthwhile consideration.

Digital

This technology has improved tremendously over recent years and it has the advantage over conventional photography that you do not require film and can load the images directly onto your computer for use on websites, send them to others directly by e-mail, or prepare coordinated and timed slide shows. Unfortunately at the time of writing the projectors required to show the images are extremely expensive.

Similarly at the moment printing A4-sized images requires higher resolution cameras and these are expensive. This will undoubtedly change, and high-quality equipment will become cheaper and more accessible.

A winter's scene quickly captured by a lightweight miniature camera carried on a sling around the neck and hung inside the breast of the jacket when not in use for quick availability. Striding Edge, Helvellyn, the Lake District

Versatile camera metering systems are vital for the ever changing face of mountain landscape photography. This shot was spot-metered on the central figure to ensure that the main point of interest was correctly exposed. A winter's day on the summit of Bowfell, the Lake District

A digital camera is just as easy to use as any point-and-shoot camera. Instead of the camera's lens projecting the image onto film it uses a CCD (Charge Coupled Device), which reacts electronically to the light and produces a pattern of coloured squares that are know as pixels. These tiny elements combine to create the whole image, and the more pixels the camera produces the higher the image quality, or resolution. The resolution of a digital camera is therefore measured by the number of pixels it produces, and is often quoted by multiplying the number of pixels across the image by the number of pixels down the image. The most basic and inexpensive digital cameras produce images of 640x480 or 350,000 pixels. The most expensive cameras are presently capable of producing images of 2048x1536 or 3.34 million pixels, often called 3.34 MegaPixel. It is not always necessary or desirable (because it eats electronic memory) to have images at a high resolution; for e-mail attachments and web page usage, lower resolution images are more than adequate.

Quality

It is my experience that you get what you pay for. But this does not mean that a basic system, relatively free from modern electronic technology, cannot give satisfactory results. Another factor to consider is the cost/weight/durability/reliability relationship. If you use your camera a lot its internal construction and mechanical parts need to be capable of taking the workload without wearing out. Additionally the body must stand the physical stresses imposed in the rough hill situation.

The lightness and convenience of a camera must be contrasted with its reliability in the field. It is no good having an ultra-sophisticated lightweight camera that cannot take the physical rigours of this branch of photography. The best advice is to go to an established and reputable dealer and rely on their knowledge and reputation to guide you.

Metering

The built-in metering system of a 35mm camera is extremely important in hillwalking photography as is the ability (as explained above) to set the aperture and shutter speeds manually if you decide to do so. The best built-in metering systems on a reflex camera measure the actual light coming *through the lens* to the film and inform the photographer what the correct settings are (shutter speed/aperture combination) to expose the film correctly. This is known as through the lens (TTL) metering. Most metering systems are *centre weighted* (see above) to give the correct exposure and this can present many problems for the photographer in the hills. (See below for an explanation on how to expose correctly with this system of metering).

The best system of metering, which only comes at a price, includes the ability of the camera to read the correct exposure only for what appears in an isolated ring seen in the centre of the eyepiece. This is known as *spot metering* and usually comes as an additional function to a centre weighted metering system. Its importance to the hillwalking photographer cannot be overemphasised, but care must be taken in selecting a camera with an advertised spot metering facility because some systems do not truly offer a single spot reading ability. Some are merely a variation on the centre weighted system and only offer an average reading with the exposure weighted in favour of a point other than the centre of the image – so take great care in selecting your camera.

THE LENS

The considerable advantage of SLR photography is that the major manufacturers offer a wide and useful range of lenses and equipment to fit any camera within their range. Check carefully whether this is the case; some manufacturers have their systems designed so that most equipment and lenses they produce will fit any of their cameras in the range. Hence it is possible to begin with a relatively cheap camera body, building up a system of lenses and so on, and when one has acquired the experience move up the range, changing the basic camera body for one offering greater sophistication. Ultimately, if a suitable system has been chosen, it may be possible to use a camera body meeting all the specifications required by the professional photographer – whilst still making use of the lenses and equipment already purchased.

Fixed Focal Length and Zoom Lenses

There are two main types of lens:

- The fixed focal length lens
- The zoom lens, where the focal length can be altered

Basically the focal length determines the width of view observed by the SLR photographer. The lens which

Lens considerations

No matter how good the camera, the lens ultimately determines the quality of image. It is pointless paying out for an optically superb lens if you only require a happy record snapshot. Conversely it is no good buying one of the many 'bargain' lenses available and expecting professional-standard sharpness. The choice is yours, but be forewarned to prevent disappointment. A useful tip when considering a lens purchase (or any camera equipment) is to read the independent tests in camera magazines. But again it is often necessary to be wary and weigh the information given with your specific needs.

This shot taken using a 28mm focal length wide angled lens places the walker centrally whilst gathering a wide panorama of hills beyond. Over the top of Pike O'Blisco to Crinkle Crags and Bowfell, the Lake District

gives the closest image to that actually seen by the eye (without the camera) is a 50mm one. A wide angle lens has a shorter focal length and gives a wider angle of view than can be seen by the naked eye. A typical wide angle lens useful to the hillwalker is 28mm. A long lens is anything above 50mm and brings a subject close in.

Theoretically a zoom lens is the perfect answer to composition, allowing any part of a scene to be selected and proportioned as the lens is adjusted. Practically, however, the zoom lens, particularly in the long focal length range above 50mm, has marked disadvantages. These include increased weight and loss of *light gathering* ability because large apertures are unavailable. Loss of light means using a slower shutter speed to expose correctly, which in turn may necessitate the use of a tripod with the corresponding loss of mobility and increase in weight. So it can be seen that choosing a lens, or system of lenses, for hillwalking photography requires careful consideration (remembering that everything used must be carried).

Practical Lens Choice

It is possible to write a book solely about lens theory and performance, but there's such a thing as too much information! So here I will look at the three lenses I use most frequently, contrasting their advantages and disadvantages and suggesting suitable alternatives.

As an indication of usefulness I offer the following breakdown of my lens use in hillwalking photography:

Wide angle	60%
Standard	35%
Long lens	5%

Wide Angle Lens

This is the most useful of all lenses to the hillwalker. I prefer a 28mm fixed focal length lens because it offers minimum distortion with good light gathering properties, but extremely good alternatives include the zoom lenses in the range 28mm to 50mm and 35mm to 70mm.

The wide angle lens is small, compact and light and, typically, will give an aperture range from f22 to f2.8. A choice of wide angle offers the advantages of fast shutter speeds, and the consequent elimination of problems with camera shake (see below), and large depth of field (see below). It allows one to get in close and still capture the whole group, and is good for the

A standard 50mm focal length lens captures a moment of rest on the magnificent traverse of the white quartzite ridges of Beinn Eighe. Torridon Mountains, North West Highlands of Scotland

expressive close-up portrait, taken on the move (remember the old press adage that there is only one rule – to get as close as possible). It is also good for landscape work to capture the overall mood of a scene.

Its disadvantages are that edge distortion does occur and this means that any verticals, say a group of trees or a perpendicular rock face, may appear 'bent' if placed near the edge of the composition. With a 28mm lens this is only a slight problem and, with due care and management, it will not detract from the photograph. The shorter the focal length (the wider the angle of the lens) the more acute is the problem, and the 24mm lens is the practical limit for hillwalking photography.

This shot, taken with a 135mm focal-length long lens, compresses the perspective to highlight the rugged mountain atmosphere. Llanberis Pass, Snowdonia, North Wales

Standard 50mm Lens

This lens offers the nearest field of view to that which the naked eye normally sees. Second to the wide angle lens it is the most useful to the hillwalker and is usually issued as standard with most cameras. It is the easiest lens to use, giving excellent quality, and the fixed focal length simplifies its use even further, making it the most suitable 'starter' lens.

Long Lens

First it should be noted how infrequently I actually use this type of lens as a percentage of my total photography. Having said this, I find that my most useful long lens, a 75mm to 150mm zoom, is invaluable for framing and capturing distant scenes. However. this type of lens has severe limitations for hillwalking photography. It is comparatively heavy, and because of this and its length it is awkward to hand hold successfully.

But in many respects the limitations imposed by size and weight are the least of the problems associated with a long lens. Firstly the light gathering properties are restricted compared with the standard or wide angle lens, and this often means a slow shutter speed is required, which in turn may necessitate the use of a tripod. Further to this the *depth of field* is very limited and it is extremely difficult to keep foregrounds in focus and the whole picture sharp. Additionally a long lens 'flattens' a scene and it is difficult to obtain any sense of perspective in the photograph.

Another practical nuisance with a long lens is the optical phenomenon whereby half of the split image (of the focusing screen) seen through the eyepiece is

Stick with it
It is always a constant source of interest to me to observe the inexperienced photographer set out with his ultra-long lens swinging on the camera strap around the neck. I suppose the initial attraction is the lens's ability to pull distant objects in close. However, most inexperienced photographers soon abandon their long lens. This is a pity because a long lens used correctly (and only practice and experience will teach its correct use) is a tremendous asset to the creative hillwalking photographer.

blacked out. This hinders correct focusing by obscuring the true lining up of the bisected image. A technique to get over this is to hold the lens steady in the same position then move your head from side to side so your eye moves across the eyepiece. In one position the blackening (a parallax effect) will disappear, enabling the image to be focused.

Framing sunsets to perfection or capturing the different evening shades, using colour or tone to replace perspective along the jagged edges of a wild mountain valley; these are just some of the uses for a long lens. Capturing distant wildlife, photographing flowers or other still life detail, and portrait work (it is generally considered that the optimum portrait lens length is 80mm) are others. But remember the limitations and note that the long lens I have found by experience to be the most practical for hillwalking photography is the 75mm to 150mm zoom.

Other Lenses

I think it prudent to note that I have always found *multiplying lenses* to be so poor in quality and restrictive in light gathering ability that I consider them to be of no practical use to the hillwalking photographer. An alternative to the awkward length of the long lens is the shorter *mirror (catadioptric)* lens, but the disadvantages are that it cannot be zoomed (an important feature in obtaining the best composition from a long lens) and that it is of a single fixed aperture so only the shutter speed can be varied to obtain correct exposure.

EQUIPMENT

Lens Hood

A lens hood should always be used because it cuts out adventitious light so enabling truer image reproduction. If not fitted as standard then collapsible rubber lens hoods can be purchased as an addition that screw into the end of the lens, and I recommend their use.

Filters

An extra weight or hindrance to the hillwalking photographer can often far outweigh any marginal benefits that extra equipment can provide. This applies even to filters, and I keep their use to an absolute minimum.

However, I fit an ultra violet (UV) or skylight filter (Wratten No.1A) as standard to all my lenses to cut haze in landscapes, giving a sharper image and better colour saturation. It also serves a very practical function in protecting the lens glass from damage in the hills. It is inexpensive to replace the filter if damaged, whereas a scratched lens is useless and must be replaced at considerable expense.

Another useful universal filter (for black and white (B&W) or colour photography) is the *polarising filter*. This only works when shooting across the sunlight (with the sun to your left or right), but can eliminate reflected glare on water or wet rocks. It can darken blue sky in some circumstances.

Use of other filters depends on whether you shoot colour or B&W film. The most practical system uses a universal holder which screws onto the end of a lens (typically the Cokin Filter System). Additionally, despite their fragility, I recommend that glass filters are used.

Filters for Black and White Photography

A *yellow filter* (Wratten No.8) darkens blue sky to a normal tone and wonderfully accentuates clouds; it also lightens foliage. A *red filter* (Wratten No.25) turns blue sky and water dark and increases contrast, particularly useful for bringing out rock features, and reduces haze.

Filters for Colour Photography

The most useful filters for the hillwalker are those which are graduated in intensity, such as a graduated neutral density (grey) filter which allows one to expose a very bright sky and dark hillside framed in one photograph correctly. Colour film, particularly colour transparency film (slide film) does not have the range of exposure that one can obtain from B&W film; therefore a graduated filter solves the very common problem of bright sky and dark landscape. Some photographers favour the use of weak reds or blues to liven up grey or flat skies.

Tripods

Only occasionally do I take a tripod out with me, but there are occasions, particularly when using a long lens, when it is essential. I use a very small, light and compact tripod, standing only 250mm high when erected. It would make most professional photographers shudder, and its use requires an athletic approach often with the photographer lying on the ground to view the subject. Of course, it is often possible to find a stone wall or boulder on which to stand this midget and this makes its use somewhat easier. If it is windy I sometimes stabilise or brace the set-up with rocks to weigh it down (I told you to use durable equipment). Do not forget to use a cable release to trigger the shutter as firing the camera directly with the hand defeats the object of using a tripod.

FILM

Type

Depth of field
This is a very important point when considering film speed. Although a faster film means, theoretically a less perfect image reproduction, it also means that a smaller aperture can be used and hence a greater *depth of field* can be achieved. The ability to achieve correct focus of the whole scene, foreground through to distant hills, is a useful one and hence the film speed decision is important and requires due consideration of the conflicting factors.

First of all you must decide just what you want from your photography. If you wish only to keep a record of your days in the hills (and there is nothing wrong with this), then the best and cheapest medium is the colour print film.

If serious about your photography, or if you wish to get your work published, then the choice is either *colour transparency film* or *black and white film*. Transparencies are difficult to view, and if they are to be shown then a projector and screen are required.

With colour and B&W photography we have two very different mediums. Often I'm asked if I find B&W photography more difficult than colour, or vice versa. It's not a question of difficulty, but of difference; they need a different approach and different techniques. Although many professionals would prefer to work in one medium at one time, it is easier not to have to constantly change one's concepts, with hill photography I often have no choice and must work in both mediums simultaneously, carrying one camera loaded with B&W and one with colour transparency film. Generally many serious photographers with their own darkroom facilities work in B&W, with the work in the darkroom being an added attraction. However the most practical and convenient medium and therefore the most popular is the colour transparency film.

Speed

Film speed is very important for the varying lighting conditions found in mountain photography. Simply put, the faster the film speed the less light is required to expose the film correctly, and therefore a faster film allows the hillwalking photographer to shoot in reduced lighting conditions.

However, the properties of film are such that faster film speeds mean greater 'grain' size and reduced clarity and quality of image. The slower the film speed the more perfect the reproduction, but this also means the brightest light (sunny clear days) is necessary to achieve the right exposure. Today, particularly with the best B&W film available, grain size is a minimal problem, and most photographers will not be able to tell the difference between the slowest and the fastest films. It all depends on what you require from your photography.

Typically *colour transparency film* is used in the range of 25 ASA to 400 ASA, with 64 ASA being probably the most generally suitable speed. I personally shoot mostly with 64 ASA and only use the slower 25 ASA when seeking to achieve the most perfect reproduction in guaranteed light conditions. I scarcely shoot with a colour transparency film greater than 100 ASA because I don't find it gives the quality I seek.

A practical B&W film speed for hillwalkers is between 50 ASA and 400 ASA. Mostly I use 125 ASA, but 400 ASA is also useful. The increase in grain size (slight in modern B&W film emulsion) in some landscape and portrait work enhances the dramatic effect of the image, and is worth experimenting with.

PHOTOGRAPHIC STORAGE

Right from the start it is essential to use a suitable storage system in which your photographs can be quickly located and viewed (and suitably protected). Even serious photographers fall down here and often end up with box upon box of excellent colour transparencies that are never viewed simply because they don't know where a particular subject is and to find it would be a major task.

If you take colour prints there are a number of reasonably priced album designs available to quickly and easily mount your photographs. For the more serious photographer who takes colour transparencies, or who wishes to store B&W negatives correctly, there are a number of suitable systems.

Probably the most convenient and least expensive system for slides is to slot them into the pockets of a transparent sleeve, usually 20 per sheet, and to hold these sheets in a ringbinder file. A fully professional

Storage conditions
Whatever system of storage you choose, it should ideally protect the photographic material from adverse physical conditions. Dust, damp and temperature problems should be eliminated with a suitably dark, dry and cool environment.

system is similar, but the sheets are larger and stored in a cabinet rather than a file. Similarly designed sheets, either paper or plastic, are available for B&W negative sheets (it is usual to cut a 36 exposure film into strips containing six shots). With B&W work it is the best practice only to make a *contact sheet,* A4 size, with all the negatives from one film exposed. This is mounted along with, and referenced to, the corresponding negative sheet. Individual images are selected from the contact and the corresponding negative is then used to make a print to the required size.

In all cases it is necessary to be able to locate the photograph required readily. This requires an organised system of storage, which does not have to be at all complicated as long as you understand it. I store my slides geographically, and if I require a slide of, say, the Pinnacle Ridge, Sgurr nan Gillean, Isle of Skye, Scotland, British Isles, then I know exactly where to look and could select a slide or negative from a variety of that particular scene taken from different viewpoints, at different times of the year, quickly and easily. The storage of B&W negative sheets is slightly more difficult because the sheets are usually made up of units of six and may contain photographs from more than one geographical location. This problem requires that the individual images are logged and cross-referenced in a book or on a computer.

TECHNIQUES IN HILLWALKING PHOTOGRAPHY

There are certain considerations of technique that are vital to successful hillwalking photography. The following I consider to be the most relevant of these and it will be seen that they are not based on a large amount of photographic theory but on sound practical experience.

Carrying Camera Gear

- Murphy's photograpic law No.1: Always carry the camera – leave it behind and you will miss the photograph of all photographs. Even if you just take a hasty, unplanned, stroll after heavy rain or as the sun begins to set, take it with you for it is often at moments such as these that the best and most interesting lighting conditions occur

- Murphy's photographic law No.2: Always have the camera easily to hand, and never turn down the opportunity of shooting a superbly lit or interesting scene thinking that the chance will occur again – it won't. Every moment in photography is unique

The practical physical considerations of carrying the camera, lenses, other gear and spare film require particularly careful attention in this field of photography. The system you employ, which must be lightweight, correctly balanced and reasonably weatherproof, must also give quick and easy access to all the photographic equipment.

I use a system – often when dangling from the end of a climbing rope – which is suitable for all the extremes of hillwalking. It consists of three stages: a bag (see picture); clipped to straps; neck strap.

This system allows the photographer freedom of movement and the minimum of hassle in carrying his equipment but, importantly, gives easy access to the camera and additional equipment during all three stages. Any photographer setting off on a hill walk of any length will find that simply carrying the camera around the neck will mean that, due to discomfort or inclement weather, the camera will eventually be relegated to the sac. The hassle of stopping, taking off the sac, taking out the camera, taking the photograph, putting back the camera and returning the sac to the back will far outweigh the enjoyment of taking the photograph. The result of carrying a camera in the sac is that it will scarcely be used.

It should also be noted that this system avoids unnecessary bulk and padding. I do not favour camera cases that are permanently attached to the camera or surround it, as they are often too heavy and restrictive, often preventing quick film replacement.

Weatherproofing

The first stage of the above system is reasonably weatherproof, but as an extra precaution against torrential rain I find the humble plastic bag invaluable. When carrying the camera around my neck (the third stage) I place it inside my jacket (sometimes inside a plastic bag) and rely on speed and dexterity to keep the camera, and the lens in particular, dry. In extreme conditions I have known people wrap the whole camera in *cling film* utilising its transparent properties to give a reasonable photograph whilst the camera is being kept dry. Watch for raindrops on the lens and wipe them away as necessary (but only if a filter protects the lens). After the walk, or when the rain stops, dry the camera (not the lens or other optical surfaces) with a suitably absorbent clean cloth or tissue.

This professional photographer has all his camera gear carried in such a fashion as to be instantly available for use. One camera is on a neck strap and one is clipped to his rucksack shoulder strap. Camera bags (where cameras can be stored should the weather turn inclement) carry alternative lens, spare film, filters and other equipment. Note also that the camera bags are located conveniently on a waist belt. Glen Sligachan, Isle of Skye, Scotland.

Cleaning the Camera and Optics

The lens should be cleaned by first using the blower brush to get rid of dust and so on, and then using a spot of lens cleaning fluid in the centre of the lens which should be removed by wiping with a tissue (not a cloth as this may scratch the lens). The wiping action is important, and should be circular in motion working from the centre to the outside of the lens. It is extremely important that the cleaning fluid is kept away from the edges of the lens as the metal/glass joint acts in capillary action sucking the fluid into the body of the lens from where it cannot be removed, and can cause permanent damage.

The eyepiece and light meter glass are best got at with a small drop of cleaning fluid and removed with a cotton wool stick. The eyepiece in particular needs frequent cleaning as it is subject to the salty perspiring face of the walker and films over, dulling the viewed image.

Cleaning the inside of a camera is a specialist job and it should be left well alone in most instances. However, it is possible that foreign bodies may be deposited on the reflecting mirror when changing lenses, and these can be removed with the blower brush. Never wipe the mirror as this can result in much damage. Although anything deposited on the mirror will be clearly seen through the eyepiece generally it will not affect the actual photographic image. This is because the mirror flips up to allow the image to reach the film when the shutter is released and the photograph taken.

In many instances the camera optics will tend to fog up with condensation, particularly with an early morning start when they have been left in the car overnight (as a first priority I take my camera gear indoors). To remove this water vapour it is necessary to raise the temperature of the camera equipment. Don't rub with a cloth or pullover sleeve but allow to air dry – I hold the independent parts up to the sun, as this quickly evaporates the water vapour. If there is no sun then body heat or the car heater also work.

SHARP PHOTOGRAPHY

Obtaining a sharp photographic image is one of the main considerations in hillwalking photography and requires the understanding and employment of a number of techniques. A sharp landscape photograph is one where all parts of the image are absolutely clear, including foreground, middleground and background. (Other photographs may be classed as sharp if only the main subject is clear, for example a fast-moving object, but in hillwalking photography this type of composition is rare.)

To achieve a sharp image:

- The lens must be focused correctly
- The camera must be held steady
- The shutter speed must be fast enough to still all movement

aperture (f4)

depth of field (8ft to infinity ∞)

Focusing

When we look through an SLR system we focus the central part of the image, so that only a part of the scene appears in focus (usually seeing this image on a split image focusing screen which is the most generally useful type of focusing screen – although more sophisticated cameras allow the type of screen to be changed).

But each lens (depending on its focal length) focuses the image both nearer and further than this centrally focused point. This property of the lens is known as *depth of field* and it is a very important factor in achieving a sharp photograph.

Depth of field, for any particular lens, depends on only one varying factor – the size of aperture. *The smaller the aperture the greater the depth of field.* Hence for this and other reasons (depending on the particular lens design) it is desirable to shoot with as

Reading the depth of field from the lens: Here the aperture of f4, set on this standard 50mm lens, gives a depth of focus from 8ft to infinity. This means that a subject some 8ft from the camera along with the mountains in the far distance (with everything in between) are in sharp focus.

small an aperture as is practical (this depends on the shutter speed because if too slow a shutter speed is used the image will be blurred due to *camera shake* – see below). Although many cameras have what is known as a 'depth of field preview button' this dulls the image to the extent that I find it singularly useless; the best means of determining depth of field is to look at the information displayed on the top of all lenses which tells you the depth of field for each focusing and aperture situation.

Having determined the depth of field information for the particular shot you are going to take, set your lens so that the maximum amount of your chosen composition is in focus. Aim to achieve sharp focus of the whole image, or if this is not possible in the prevailing light conditions then ensure that the main subjects are in focus. It should be the aim of any landscape photograph to correctly focus both the foreground and the distant mountains. Therefore the lens must be set accordingly. In a well-lit scene it is possible to set the lens so that everything in the composition is in sharp focus, from the foreground (typically a cairn only 3m in front of the photographer) to infinity. Alternatively, if you wish to focus only a part of the image (say a figure or object which is to be the whole point of the photograph) then the depth of field should be set to focus solely on this one distant point.

Shutter Speed and Camera Shake

Avoiding camera shake
A very useful rule of thumb to avoid the effects of camera shake is to make *the shutter speed at least equal to the focal length* of the lens being used.

It is essential to hold the camera steady enough to obtain a clear image. The pictures here illustrate the correct way to hold the camera as steady as possible.

Of course shutter speed plays a vital role in avoiding the effects of *camera shake*. Photographers have beating hearts and expanding and contracting lungs, and move their hands and arms to some extent even when they think they are perfectly still. All photographers can effectively avoid camera shake by shooting at 1/250 of a second. Most will be fine shooting at 1/125. With care and holding the camera steady, as shown on p.147, 1/60 is a practical speed at which to shoot enabling a small aperture to be used and therefore giving great depth of field.

Shooting with slow shutter speeds requires careful concentration and it helps to hold your breath to still most body movement. I'm lucky in that I have very steady hands and using the above techniques have successfully shot, without tripod, with shutter speeds lower than 1/60.

Holding the camera correctly for normal conditions:
the camera is held to the eye firmly and in such a manner that the arms are braced tight to the body for maximum rigidity. Here the photograph is being framed horizontally (see Composition) but the points made apply equally to vertical framing. Keep the fingers away from the front of the lens, hold the camera body and release the shutter with one hand, focus and support the lens with the other.

Steadying the camera on a wall or boulder:
here the base of the camera rests horizontally on a convenient wall or boulder.

Using the knees for increased stability:
here the technique is much the same as before but if no other means of support is available, as is often the case on a steep hillside, or if the photograph must be taken immediately then the stability provided by using the knees whilst sitting is a useful practical way to take a shot requiring slow shutter speeds.

Steadying a long lens on a wall or boulder: using a long lens often requires the stability provided by supporting the barrel or tip of the lens in addition to the base of the camera. Because of the irregular nature of walls and boulders it is by no means easy to do both but it can be done using a hand braced as necessary beneath the camera body as illustrated here. If only one point of contact can be made (equipment to rock) then support the lens in preference to the camera body to facilitate the desire framing.

Capturing Movement

In hillwalking photography there isn't a great deal of rapid movement, unless you happen to spot a fellrunner or wild animal running by, and a shutter speed of 1/250 will still most movement (1/500 serves as a practical maximum figure). However, it may be desirable to capture walking movement and to give the feel of mobility in a photograph. The technique to achieve this, where the central moving subject (the walker) is sharp and clear and the background blurred (giving the impression of movement and at the same time accentuating the main subject) is called *panning the camera*. This simply involves following the movement by swinging the camera with the subject as he moves along – a continuous and smooth action is required and – of course – plenty of practice.

A further sophistication of this technique, and that of stilling movement with shutter speed, involves the effect of differential movement velocities. Panning a fast-moving object gives the above effect and can be achieved at surprisingly low shutter speeds, and so it is possible to still a walker's body, with background blurred, and also to blur (to a lesser extent than the background) his fast-moving parts, that is, the legs and arms. The effects are interesting and it is really up to the individual to try these techniques out for himself. Of course it should be appreciated that these are mere nuances in technique and should be treated as such.

It can be seen then that the sharp photography depends on both focusing and shutter speed. Although there are many considerations involved in obtaining the desired image, those starting out should strive to

Movement captured by slow shutter speed: a waterfall shot with a shutter speed of 1/4 of a second.

Movement stilled by fast shutter speed: the same scene shot with a shutter speed of 1/250 of a second. The water here is, rather artificially, stilled with individual droplets frozen in mid-air.

achieve a fully focused and unblurred photograph – this is the starting point for further photography and is a position that some photographers never attain!

USING THE LIGHT

Light is everything in photography, not only because no light means no photograph, but because understanding, appreciating, manipulating and capturing optimum lighting elevates a photograph above the status of mere image reproduction. In a studio the photographer controls his environment and adjusts the light at the flick of a switch. On the hills the light changes every year, every season, every day and virtually every minute. The great art, and thrill, in hillwalking photography is being in the right place at the right time, with the ability to recognise and use the light to create an inspiring and satisfying photograph. To do this one must have an understanding of the seasons and the time of day and the ability to expose the presented image correctly.

Exposure and Metering

The correct amount of light must be exposed onto the film to produce satisfactory results. This is decided by the metering and the best system of metering, in this field of photography, is built into the camera (and the most suitable of built-in metering systems has a spot metering facility). Using the metering system satisfactorily requires experience and if spot metering isn't available, especially if using colour film which has a much narrower exposure range than B&W film, it is necessary to meter (view) certain sections of a

Flowing water

One aspect of hillwalking photography involving subject movement and the different images to be captured by different shutter speed selection is capturing flowing water, typically falling in a mountain waterfall. To give the water a super-smooth silky effect use a shutter speed of one quarter of a second (a tripod is necessary). To give the flow a more realistic effect, use 1/30, and to freeze even individual droplets shoot at 1/250 or above.

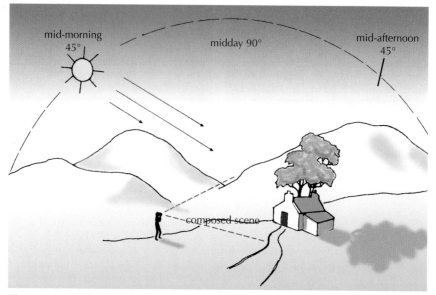

Photographer looking across sunlight with the sun positioned low in the sky to provide interesting contrast to the scene. this is most effectively achieved with the sun at around 45° in the sky when the effects of light and shade produce interesting contrasts.

Positioning oneself between the sun and the object to be photographed: the first simple rule of light is most useful when photographing an individual walker or group. It requires a certain degree of energy and mobility in the photographer to capture a fast-moving party but it always repays the effort.

landscape above and beyond what may actually be the final composition. For example, when taking a landscape shot with foreground, mountain and sky with a centre weighted system, which is the norm in most SLR cameras, it is often no use composing the scene reading the meter (and adjusting aperture and shutter speed accordingly) then shooting. Most often this will simply overexpose the sky and underexpose the foreground.

To beat this, one must first decide which part of the scene one wishes to expose correctly, and to what degree. It may be desirable to expose the sky correctly, leaving mountain and valley underexposed (darker). First point the camera solely at the sky, read the meter and adjust the settings accordingly, then compose and focus the scene to be photographed. Obviously different degrees of exposure may be desirable and it is up to the photographer to quantify these as necessary but using the above basic technique to get the best from the meter.

Any system of metering can easily be wrong in the complex scenes often composed in landscape photography, especially if rippling water forms part of the subject. Producing the desired results here is a matter of experience and, even for the most experienced and proficient of hillwalking photographers, to some degree a matter of luck. Most employ a system known as *bracketing the exposure* which for a given shutter speed means first exposing the scene at the setting you think is best, and then taking two further shots with the aperture first open and then closed two further stops from the first shot. This first shot is then effectively bracketed by two differently exposed shots in the hope that one of the three will be satisfactory.

Lastly, always have regard to the manufacturer's simple exposure guide which is issued with every film (that piece of paper you all throw straight in the bin). It will simply recommend a shutter speed and aperture setting for, say, four different lighting conditions (for example, bright sun, blue sky shutter speed 1/125 with aperture f16). Recalling this memorised information adds a sound sense of perspective and can pay dividends when deciding on a suitable exposure setting even when the meter and all the above techniques are used.

To under- or over-expose?

It is generally better to under- than overexpose, and some professionals do this to achieve better colour saturation, relying on corrective developing to achieve correct exposure. This can be achieved in a number of ways depending on your particular camera, but some photographers move the film speed setting along to the next fastest speed, for example if the actual film used was 64 ASA then the film speed indicator could be moved to 80 ASA. These are subtle tricks, but only tricks, and should be recognised as such. For those with any doubts on the difficult subject of exposure, as with all aspects of photography, it is always better to master the basic techniques first.

Shooting into the sun

This is the most difficult way to use light. Some professional photographers will not risk wasting a shot by doing this, yet it can produce the most exciting results. Capturing a sunrise, sunset or the intriguing effect of a moonscape are the most obvious examples of shooting into the sun (or more accurately, directly into sunlight). But there are other effects to be sought by the adventurous photographer, such as the effect known as *starbreak* which can look superbly stunning when suitably composed with a further point of interest, such as a figure or mountain ridge. Here the photographer composes the scene directly into the sun and uses a reasonably small aperture with a reasonably quick speed. Try f11 at 1/500 with a standard lens and film speed of 64 ASA – but experiment to achieve the desired results.

The Right Place

Being in the right place really means being there at the right time! I am of course talking about capturing the optimum lighting conditions and this depends largely on the juxtaposition of you and the sun. The sun's position overhead is dependent on both the time of year and the time of day.

The hillwalking photographer will seek to know this basic information and place himself in the right place at the right time to achieve the desired results. Early mornings and evenings can give the most marvellous and dramatic sky scenes imaginable and if these can be captured, along with the outline form of some dramatic peak, then the hillwalking photographer should forget about the hours kept by ordinary mortals, and leave his bed early only to return after dark.

However, the main part of the day, naturally, provides the easiest and most reliable lighting conditions. Typically these occur between 10.00am and 4.00pm in summer and, generally, it is then that the hillwalking photographer may achieve the clearest results. However, when the sun is directly overhead, and the shadows non-existent, there is little contrast and many landscape scenes will appear completely flat when photographed.

I will give some guidelines and tips on how the time of day and the position of the sun and the photographer affect the image quality. Whilst a few simple rules will do much to enable you to be in the right place at the right time, however, one must experiment with and use the light to understand its effects.

One of the very first rules of outdoor photography is to shoot with the sun behind so that the scene being photographed is fully lit. When photographing a group or other reasonably static object, it is up to the photographer to place himself between the image and the sun.

Another favourable lighting situation for landscape work, is when the sun is at 45 degrees over the left or right shoulder and this will provide suitable contrast to give interest to the image.

The Right Time

Photographing at the right time means being at the *right place* at the right time. This means when the sun is in its optimum position in the sky for the type of photograph required, when the weather is favourable and when using the correct techniques for the prevailing season of the year.

Each season of the year has its own beauty and attractions:

- Summer is the most popular photographic season, but for many reasons it is not always the easiest or most satisfying
- Spring can offer much clearer air, free from the heat hazes often affecting summer
- Autumn can offer the most wonderful colours as the leaves change and fall and the bracken reddens to the colour of blood
- Winter brings the hoar frost crystals and white snows, smoothing all those jagged outlines into smooth contours

However, I think it is prudent to outline some of the light and exposure problems that may occur throughout these seasons and give some indication of how to overcome them.

An example of starbreak (see opposite) when the shot is taken directly into the sun above the jagged peaks and appears as a spectacular spangled star in the resultant image. Starbreak captured over the Chamonix Aiguille, French Alps

Haze

Midsummer is the worst time for this problem. Its effects can be somewhat reduced by use of a filter, and it can be avoided to some extent by shooting during the cooler times of day.

Wet Misty Conditions

It will surprise most people but these conditions can give excellent photographic results if the subject is chosen wisely. The meter will inevitably show that there is more light than you would expect. Try detail shots, say of a walker kitted out in bright waterproofs. These conditions produce *diffused light* and colour saturation can be markedly improved.

Snow on the Ground

The reflective qualities of snow and ice will most often fool the light meter, showing the scene to be brighter than it really is. To expose snow correctly it is usual to increase the aperture by one or two stops. Also don't worry if your colour transparencies show the apparently white snow to be blue. That most probably will be its true colour – likewise ice can vary in colour from blue to green.

Clear Air at Altitude

If walking in the Alps or elsewhere at altitude it is

surprising just how the lack of water vapour in the air brightens the scene; so much so that it is imperative to use the slowest film speed available (25 ASA) to achieve the correct exposures. Also it is worth noting the effects of filters reducing the amount of light reaching the film (particularly useful is the polarising filter).

COMPOSITION

It is a fact that certain images seen by the eye please the brain more than others. These images were understood and used by the great Classical artists. If the image is composed in certain ways then it becomes infinitely more interesting and attractive.

A skilled artist with brush and canvas can compose the painting exactly as he chooses. The hillwalking photographer has a much more problematical job composing the components of the real world to obtain a good photograph. However, it can be achieved and when the gifted photographer portrays a natural scene he is reflecting an infinitely wonderful natural world to its best effect and is producing a work of art as fine as any created on canvas.

There are a few simple points and rules of composition which will greatly enhance the photograph.

Central Subject

The first simple rule of composition to understand is to centralise the main subject of interest. If you are photographing Uncle Fred walking along on his holidays nothing else matters greatly, so get him in the dead centre of the frame – the central point of interest.

It should be noted that the view seen through the eyepiece of a camera which is not an SLR is not exactly the image that will be imposed on the film. Although most non-SLRs are reasonably accurate the individual displacement, for each camera, should be appreciated to avoid cutting off Uncle Fred's feet or head.

Rule of Thirds

The most useful composition to the landscape or hillwalking photographer involves an understanding of what I call the rule of thirds. If the scene is mentally divided into three sections both horizontally and vertically then the intersection points (third points) are the points that most catch the eye and are therefore the points at which to place the subjects of interest.

Note, however, that the whole image is a question

of balance and, typically, the eye should be led into the photograph along a track or with a lesser point of interest to counterbalance the main subject in the opposite third.

A further point to appreciate with the above rule of thirds is that the plane along the lines themselves is known as the *golden section* and is the place to situate any straight vertical or horizontal lines that may run through the photograph. Wherever possible straight lines through a composition should be avoided as they tend to reduce its interest as a whole (for example, a boat jetty running horizontally across a photograph will separate and alienate the material below from that above and should be avoided). However, in landscape work they are often unavoidable.

Other Points on Composition

There are numerous other points that deserve some individual mention, and these are frequently stumbling blocks to those unaware of their importance.

Horizontal and Vertical Lines

Certain straight lines should ideally be seen as either horizontal or vertical. If the scene involves a flat area of water, a large lake or the sea, then remember that the distant shoreline should be placed horizontally in the composition. Trees or vertical walls should also be seen to be vertical, otherwise the image will just not satisfy the brain which knows these things are always so.

Competing Points of Interest

Avoid dual points of interest; the brain does not like clutter and they can considerably detract from the enjoyment of a photograph. However, there are occasions when an unwanted subject cannot be removed from the composition (electricity and telegraph lines are particularly infuriating). In a case like this I find the best solution is to make a feature out of the offending object.

Detail

Sometimes it is very difficult to understand just how to capture the true magic of the moment, for example all the colours of an autumn scene can be intoxicating, but when photographed collectively the result can be disappointing, and the photograph does not live up to expectations. An answer to this is to go for the general to the specific and *concentrate on detail*. Capture those

Using scale (see next page) – this shot taken using a 28mm focal-length wide-angled lens keeps the foreground figure of the walker small in comparison to the distant snow-clad peaks beyond. The effect is to dramatically accentuate the apparent size of the mountains. Over Wast Water to Scafell, the Lake District.

The central composition: here the photograph is composed with the main point of interest placed centrally. Avoid cutting off any bits of this main subject as this considerably spoils the image. The Matterhorn above Zermatt, Switzerland

Balancing the composition: a well composed photograph employs the rule of thirds and is also well balanced. It is good technique to use an object of lesser interest placed in the lower third to lead the viewer into the photo and to balance the stronger point of interest (a mountain peak for example) placed opposite in the upper third. Along the Blea Tarn road to Side Pike with the Langdale Pikes beyond, the Lake District

The rule of thirds: this shows the position to place the main points of interest. Over the Sligachan Inn down Glen Sligachan to Marsco, Red Cuillin, Isle of Skye, Scotland

dead brown leaves floating forlornly in the mountain pool, a tiny composition but one that says unmistakably, 'This is autumn'.

Scale

Mention must be made of scale as this is an important point to be appreciated by the hillwalking photographer. If one wishes to show just how high those mountains were that you climbed then it helps if you can accentuate the effect using the concept of scale. Keep the object in the foreground small – a tree or rock or walker – with the mountains rising dramatically above dwarfing the foreground.

Framing Vertically or Horizontally

This is worth a bit of thought. The image made by the 35mm format camera is rectangular. If the camera is held normally then the image is framed horizontally (with the longest side of the rectangle horizontal); turned through 90 degrees the camera frames the image vertically (the longest side of the rectangle is then vertical). Vertical framing is often the best way to capture hill and mountain scenes, giving a real concept of depth.

CONCLUSION

The subject of hillwalking photography is wide, that of general photography vast, and I have merely highlighted the most important practical points here. I started with a passion, then I learnt something of what I was about. You will do it your way but I say, in all seriousness, first learn the rules then you can break them – that's where the fun begins. For me, as it was in the beginning, the passion remains, as does the joy of learning.

Enjoy your hillwalking, try photography, but above all be safe and caring on those magnificent hills.

APPENDIX

Useful Names and Addresses

General

ASSOCIATION OF
NATIONAL PARKS
Ponsford House
Moretonhampstead
Devon TQ13 8NL
Tel 01647 440 245
www.ANPA.gov.uk

ASSOCIATION FOR AONBs
The Old Police Station
Cotswold Heritage Centre
Northleach
Gloucestershire GL54 3JH
Tel: 01451 862 007
www.aonb.org.uk

BRITISH MOUNTAINEERING
COUNCIL
177-179 Burton Road
West Didsbury
Manchester M20 2BB
Tel: 0161 445 4747
www.thebmc.co.uk

CNP – COUNCIL
FOR NATIONAL PARKS
246 Lavender Hill
London, SW11 1LJ
Tel: 020 7924 4077
Email: info@cnp.org.uk

FRIENDS OF THE EARTH
26-28 Underwood Street
London N1 7JQ
Tel: 020 7490 1555
www.foe.co.uk

GREENPEACE UK
Canonbury Villas
London W1 2PN
Tel: 020 7865 8100
www.greenpeace.org.uk

HARVEY MAPS
12-22 Main Street
Doune
Perthshire FK16 6BJ
Tel: 01786 841202
www.harveymaps.co.uk

JOHN MUIR TRUST
41 Commercial Street
Leith
Edinburgh EH6 6JD
Tel: 0131 554 0114
www.jmt.org

THE OPEN SPACES SOCIETY
25A Bell Street
Henley-on-Thames
Oxon RG9 2BA
Tel: 01491 573 535
www.oss.org.uk

MOUNTAIN
BOTHIES ASSOCIATION
18 Castle View, Airth
Stirlingshire FK2 8GE
Tel: 01324 832 700

MOUNTAIN LEADER
TRAINING BOARD
Siabod Cottage
Capel Curig
Conwy LL24 OET
Tel: 01690 720 248
www.mltb.org

ORDNANCE SURVEY
Romsey Road
Maybush
Southampton SO16 4GU
Tel: 023 8079 2912
www.ordsv.gov.uk

ROYAL SOCIETY FOR THE
PROTECTION OF BIRDS
(RSPB)
The Lodge
Sandy
Bedfordshire SG19 2DL
Tel: 01767 680 551
www.rspb.org.uk

Regional

England:

COUNCIL FOR THE
PROTECTION OF RURAL
ENGLAND
Warwick House
25 Buckingham Palace Road
London SW1W OPP
Tel: 020 7976 6373
Email: cpre@gn.apc.org

THE COUNTRYSIDE
AGENCY
John Dower House
Crescent Place
Cheltenham
Gloucestershire GL50 3RA
Tel: 01242 521381
www.countryside.gov.uk

NATIONAL TRUST
36 Queen Anne's Gate
London SW1H 9AS
Tel: 020 7222 9251
www.nationaltrust.org.uk

THE RAMBLERS'
ASSOCIATION
2nd Floor Camelford House
87-90 Albert Embankment
London SE1 7TW
Tel: 020 7339 8585
www.ramblers.org.uk

Northern Island:

DEPARTMENT OF THE
ENVIRONMENT,
TRANSPORT AND THE
REGIONS
Environment and
Heritage Service
35 Caslte Street
Belfast BT1 1GU
Tel: 028 9054 6553

Scotland:

MOUNTAINEERING
COUNCIL OF SCOTLAND
The Old Granary
West Mill Street
Perth PH1 5QP
Tel: 01738 638 227
www.mountaineering
-scotland.org.uk

NATIONAL TRUST FOR
SCOTLAND
Wemyss House
28 Charlotte Square
Edinburgh EH2 4ET
Tel: 0131 243 9300
www.nts.org.uk

RAMBLERS ASSOCIATION
SCOTLAND
Kingfisher House
Auld Mart Business Park
Milnathort, Kinross
Fife
KY 13
Tel: 01577 861221
www.ramblers.org.uk

SCOTTISH NATURAL
HERITAGE
12 Hope Terrace
Edinburgh EH9 2AS
Tel: 0131 447 4784
www.snh.org.uk

SCOTTISH RIGHTS OF WAY
AND ACCESS SOCIETY
24 Annandale Street
Edinburgh EH7 4AN
Tel: 0131 558 1222
www.scotways.demon.co.uk

SCOTTISH WILD LAND
GROUP
8 Hartington Place
Bruntsfield
Edinburgh EH10 4LE
Tel: 0131 229 2094

Wales:

COUNCIL FOR
THE PROTECTION
OF RURAL WALES
Ty Gwyn, 31 High Street
Welshpool, Pows SY21 7YD
Tel: 01938 552 525
Email: yvcw@aol.com

COUNTRYSIDE
COUNCIL FOR WALES
Plas Gogerddan
Aberystwyth
Ceredigion SY23 3EE
Tel: 01970 828 551
www.ccw.gov.uk

Cicerone's mission is to inform and inspire by providing the best guides to exploring the world

Since its foundation over 30 years ago, Cicerone has specialised in publishing guidebooks and has built a reputation for quality and reliability. It now publishes nearly 300 guides to the major destinations for outdoor enthusiasts, including Europe, UK and the rest of the world.

Written by leading and committed specialists, Cicerone guides are recognised as the most authoritative. They are full of information, maps and illustrations so that the user can plan and complete a successful and safe trip or expedition – be it a long face climb, a walk over Lakeland fells, an alpine traverse, a Himalayan trek or a ramble in the countryside.

With a thorough introduction to assist planning, clear diagrams, maps and colour photographs to illustrate the terrain and route, and accurate and detailed text, Cicerone guides are designed for ease of use and access to the information.

If the facts on the ground change, or there is any aspect of a guide that you think we can improve, we are always delighted to hear from you.

Cicerone Press
2 Police Square Milnthorpe Cumbria LA7 7PY
Tel:01539 562 069   Fax:01539 563 417
e-mail:info@cicerone.co.uk   web:www.cicerone.co.uk

CICERONE